The Illuminati Tarot

The Illuminati Tarot
Keys of Secret Societies

Casey DuHamel

Illustrated by Bob Greyvenstein

4880 Lower Valley Road • Atglen, PA 19310

Copyright © 2017 by Casey DuHamel and Bob Greyvenstein

Library of Congress Control Number: 2016958431

All rights reserved. No part of this work may be reproduced or used in any form or by any means—graphic, electronic, or mechanical, including photocopying or information storage and retrieval systems—without written permission from the publisher.

The scanning, uploading, and distribution of this book or any part thereof via the Internet or any other means without the permission of the publisher is illegal and punishable by law. Please purchase only authorized editions and do not participate in or encourage the electronic piracy of copyrighted materials.

"Schiffer," "Schiffer Publishing, Ltd.," and the pen and inkwell logo are registered trademarks of Schiffer Publishing, Ltd.

Concept design and box layout created by Matthew Goodman | Designed by Danielle Farmer
Type set in Worn Manuscript/Historical/CaslonAntiqueEF

ISBN: 978-0-7643-5270-6 | Printed in China

Published by Schiffer Publishing, Ltd.
4880 Lower Valley Road
Atglen, PA 19310
Phone: (610) 593-1777; Fax: (610) 593-2002
E-mail: Info@schifferbooks.com
Web: www.schifferbooks.com

For our complete selection of fine books on this and related subjects, please visit our website at www.schifferbooks.com. You may also write for a free catalog.

Schiffer Publishing's titles are available at special discounts for bulk purchases for sales promotions or premiums. Special editions, including personalized covers, corporate imprints, and excerpts, can be created in large quantities for special needs. For more information, contact the publisher.

We are always looking for people to write books on new and related subjects. If you have an idea for a book, please contact us at proposals@schifferbooks.com.

Other Schiffer Books
on Related Subjects

TAROT SPREADS AND LAYOUTS: A USER'S MANUAL FOR BEGINNING AND INTERMEDIATE READERS. Jeanne Fiorini. ISBN: 978-0-7643-3629-4

TAROT, RITUALS & YOU: THE POWER OF TAROT COMBINED WITH THE POWER OF RITUAL. Bonnie Cehovet. ISBN: 978-0-7643-4318-6

TAROT—UNLOCKING THE ARCANA. Angelo Nasios. ISBN: 978-0-7643-5037-5

FRATERNALLY YOURS: IDENTIFY FRATERNAL GROUPS AND THEIR EMBLEMS. Peter Swift Seibert. ISBN: 978-0-7643-4060-4

NOTE: The suit of Coins is numerated with Arabic numbers, not Roman numerals, as the original Martinist Tarot deck was done.

Contents

8
Chapter One:
Tripping the Royal Road

16
Chapter Two:
Within These Hallowed Halls

23
Chapter Three:
The Cards

37
Chapter Four:
The Priory of Sion

41
Chapter Six:
The Major Arcana

The Fool 42
The Magician I 45
    The High Priestess II 48
The Empress III 51
The Emperor IIII 54
The Hierophant V 57
The Lovers VI 60
The Chariot VII 63
Justice VIII 66
The Hermit VIIII 69
The Wheel of Fortune X 72

Strength XI 75
The Hanged Man XII 78
Death XIII 81
Temperance XIII 84
The Devil XV 87
The Tower XVI 90
The Star XVII 93
The Moon XVIII 96
The Sun XVIIII 99
Judgement XX 102
The World XXI 105

109
Chapter Seven:
Minor Arcana

Cups

The Rosicrucians 110
Novice of Cups 112
Initiate of Cups 114

Adept of Cups 116
Mage of Cups 118
The Pips 120

Ace of Cups 121	Ace of Wands....................153
Two of Cups 121	Two of Wands 153
Three of Cups 122	Three of Wands.................154
Four of Cups 122	Four of Wands 154
Five of Cups 123	Five of Wands 155
Six of Cups 123	Six of Wands.....................155
Seven of Cups...................124	Seven of Wands 156
Eight of Cups 124	Eight of Wands 156
Nine of Cups 125	Nine of Wands 157
Ten of Cups.......................125	Ten of Wands 157

COINS   SWORDS

The Martinists 126	**The Freemasons....................158**
Novice of Coins 128	Novice of Swords 160
Initiate of Coins 130	Initiate of Swords 162
Adept of Coins..................132	Adept of Swords................164
Mage of Coins 134	Mage of Swords................166
The Pips...............................136	**The Pips...............................168**
Ace of Coins 137	Ace of Swords 169
Two of Coins 137	Two of Swords..................169
Three of Coins 138	Three of Swords 170
Four of Coins....................138	Four of Swords.................170
Five of Coins 139	Five of Swords..................171
Six of Coins 139	Six of Swords 171
Seven of Coins 140	Seven of Swords 172
Eight of Coins...................140	Eight of Swords 172
Nine of Coins....................141	Nine of Swords 173
Ten of Coins 141	Ten of Swords 173

WANDS

The Golden Dawn 142	
Novice of Wands 144	
Initiate of Wands................146	
Adept of Wands 148	
Mage of Wands 150	
The Pips...............................152	

174
Conclusion

175
Bibliography

Chapter One

Tripping the Royal Road

Known as "The Royal Road," this cryptic system of seventy-eight cards boasts a complicated history that evokes enthusiastic debate and discourse among today's Tarot aficionados. Indications as to how these cards became celebrated as The Royal Road is vague, the most ubiquitous interpretation being the sequence represents the way to wisdom. Some believe the word "tarot" is comprised of the two Egyptian words, "tar" meaning royal and "ot" meaning road—the Royal Road. This belief is based on the fanciful interpretations of Antoine Court de Gébelin, an eighteenth-century French Freemason and the first to apply occult meaning to the Tarot. The meaning of "occult" must be properly understood in this regard. Other than meaning secret or hidden, Western occultism refers to a permutation of gnosticism, alchemy, astrology, numerology, and Judeo-Christian mysticism that became intertwined during the Renaissance, then infiltrated the esoteric fraternities of eighteenth–nineteenth century France. This occult movement crossed the English Channel in the late 1800s, thanks in large part to the correspondence between renowned hermeticians such as England's A. E. Waite and France's Eliphas Levi. Western occultism became ensconced within Victorian society, flourishing in England and Scotland's hermetic lodges, then eventually making its way across the Atlantic Ocean to North America where it continues to thrive to this day.

Concerning the cards' origins, recent research by grail scholars, such as Margaret Starbird, Malcolm Godwin, and Graham Phillips, and Tarot experts, such as Christine Payne-Towler, Robert M. Place, Mary K. Greer, and Rachel Pollack, has provided readily available volumes chock full of solid theory and valid concepts. The Internet provides one with a cornucopia of Tarot information ranging from the mundane to the exemplary and exceptional. It is accepted in Tarot academia that the French word "tarot" derives from the Italian *tarocchi*, which has no known etymology. Many believe "tarot" has its roots in Arabic, which sustains validity. "Tarot" is very similar to the Arabic word طرق (*turuq*), which means "four ways." According to French etymology, the Italian *tarocco* derives from the Arabic طرح (*ṭarḥ*): rejection, subtraction, deduction, discount (terms which could apply to early Italian trick-taking games such as trionfi). The word may be related to Harut and Marut, two angels mentioned in the Qur'an. According to this account, a group of Israelites were bequeathed the art of magic from the two angels. It may be more than coincidence there is a phonetic resemblance between the word "tarot" تورات, Harut توراه, and Marut تورام.

History is a double-edged sword; accounts are written by the victors. The losers have a completely different story to tell, one which is just as valid but known only to the few. To find these narratives requires a bit more digging and a bit of postulation. This edge of the sword is known as alternative history and the completed picture is surprisingly obvious when the puzzle pieces have been sorted and completed into one comprehensive image. To use a well-worn *bon mot*, we have not been able to see the forest through the trees. When dealing with subject matter of such immense scope, there is a risk of oversimplifying the issues. By employing the principle of Occam's Razor (the simplest solution is most often correct), the over-growth of minutiae is discarded and a glimpse of the forest may be viewed with open eyes.

Arabic Origins

It has been established modern playing cards, in all probability, emerged from the gambling games of ancient Muslim society. Mamluks, soldiers drafted from the slave caste, converted to Islam and served the Muslim caliphs and the Ayyubid sultans during the Middle Ages. Over time, they evolved into a powerful military social order. The Islamic Mamluks seized the Egypt sultanate in 1250, a period which lasted until 1517. This fact may account for the idea occult Tarot originated in dynastic Egypt. Tarot aficionados can rest assured the Tarot did not originate in Egypt during this period or any other period—this is clearly a matter of production and mistaken attribution. Tarots are cards therefore printed on paper. Paper is an invention that originated in second century China where it stayed until the mid-eighth century. The material was used as an inexpensive alternative to silk and eventually for a type of playing card or money card. Ancient Egyptians did not have this paper-making technology, utilizing papyrus as a medium instead. Paper-making was introduced into Middle Eastern and eventually European culture by way of Muslim infiltration. Following the battle of Tallas (751 CE), which was fought between the Chinese and Muslim forces, Chinese prisoners revealed the secret of paper-making. Islamic craftsmen turned the Chinese art form into a major industry. Arab society may have been enjoying playing cards as early as the 1100s as there are accounts of the Chinese playing a game utilizing domino-type cards in 969 CE. The Mamluk cards were hand-painted playing cards with suits relevant to Muslim society: coins, cups, scimitars, and polo-sticks (polo being the earliest known team sport and originating in Persia).

It is not unreasonable to assume these playing cards flourished in Muslim-occupied Spain—Al Andalus (710–1492). Medieval Spain, known as the Iberian Peninsula, was the scene of constant warfare between the occupying Muslims and Spanish/French Christians. Surely, during seven hundred years' time, Iberian and French society became aware of the Muslim playing cards. Templar Knights, returning to France from the Crusades, may have brought the Muslim gaming cards with them, procured during direct contact with Islamic forces. Although feasible, there is no existing evidence to support this presumption. It is possible the original Arabic gambling game may have been absorbed into south-western France through the shared border of the Barcelonan buffer zone. Barcelona was, and is, the capital of Catalonia, which precariously separated the Muslim Al-Andalus from France. This theory is not altogether impossible and may carve out an entirely different fork in the Royal Road.

Oui, Oui!

It is accepted as fact Tarot cards were not born within the initiatic halls of Egyptian mystery schools; their illustrious birth was not engraved upon temple columns in ancient Egypt. Another myth dispelled is Tarot was brought into medieval Mediterranean Europe by the nomadic gypsy culture, which arrived in Europe years earlier from the Indian subcontinent. Again, this is a matter of production and mistaken identity. The cards were very costly to produce in medieval Europe and a pastime favorite among the upper classes. Gypsy tribes were nomadic, indigent, and often worked as slaves. Lacking the technology, this ethnic caste would not have been able to produce playing cards nor would they have had the resources to procure them. Therefore, it is doubtful Tarots arrived in Europe with the influx of gypsies. This theory may have its beginnings in eighteenth-century France promulgated by the father of Tarot divination, Etteilla, who created and published a Tarot deck known as *The Tarot of the Gypsies*. It was believed then that gyp-sies had originated in the land of E-gyp-t, an erroneous application of etymology. Even though gypsies were and are those most often associated with fortune-telling, the foundation of divination with playing cards is historically placed in 1700s France. The gypsy fable is dismissed when one considers the cards existed in Europe prior to the appearance of gypsies on the continent.

It has been established suited card gaming was conceived by ancient Muslim culture originating with the Mamluks. It is logical to assume the shared border of medieval Spain and southern France would allow for the assimilation of Muslim game cards into French culture where they would have evolved and been modified to reflect French society. By the late 1200s, many Islamic Iberian territories were eradicated from Spain by Christian armies, but surely many of their traditions remained, including gaming cards. These gambling amusements were deemed by the church to be corruption and eventually outlawed in Spain by ecclesiastical decree in

1382. France followed in her neighbor's footsteps, applying the same delegation shortly thereafter. The cards soon resurfaced in northern Italy where they flourished artistically in the noble courts influenced by the open-minded sophistication of the early Renaissance. It is interesting to note Spain has not published a Tarot deck since its early decree in 1382 until the modern age—1900!

The concept is reasonable and rational; it is logical to accept the notion Tarot has its roots firmly planted in ancient Arabic gaming cards. It is also logical to assume these Arabic decks made contact with Europe by way of Spain and France. Following this train of thought: what if the word "tarot" did not derive from the Italian *tarocchi* (which has no known etymological history), but that *tarocchi* in effect stemmed from the French word *tarot*, which it has been shown very possibly has Arab linguistic roots. That simple notion has far reaching implications. Such a statement would indicate Tarot did not originate in northern Italy and flow northward, disseminating throughout the continent; it would suggest European Tarot maintains a French heritage born as early as the thirteenth century, before the Avignon Papacy. The chivalric suited card game that originated with the Muslims would have been modified, depicting French society with the addition of extra court cards (including queens; the appearance of queens in Muslim decks would have been an affront to the tenets of Islam) and a change of suit symbols: polo sticks became scepters or batons, cups came to resemble chalices, scimitars became the more traditional European sword, and coins became the French monetary. The early French decks would then have numbered fifty-six cards. There are proponents supporting the theory of Tarot's genesis in France. It is thought by many scholars the proto-Tarots actually hailed from the Marseille district of southern France during years spanning the late 1200s to the late 1300s. This region is profoundly significant when referring to Christian heresy: Black Madonnas, cult of St. Sarah, the veneration of Mary Magdalene, and Les Trois Maries (the three Marys—Mary Magdalene, Mary of Clopas, and Mary Salome—and their arrival on Marseille shores in an oarless boat; some accounts say without sails or rudder as well).Tarot scholar, author, and Cabalist Isabel Radow Kliegman says: "A more scholarly approach would say that Tarot first appeared in thirteenth-century France, in the still-available Marseilles deck."

During the 1200s–mid-1300s, an extraordinary thing may have occurred in France that would have coincided with the annihilation of the last surviving

Cathars in the Languedoc region, residing in the southeastern provinces of the country. These innocuous decks of playing cards may have morphed into something entirely different. They may have been paired with an iconography of twenty-two mysterious paper pictograms, created in France by an unknown author, possibly a clergyman well versed in Gnosticism and sacred geometry, as camouflaged icons that perhaps celebrated the Cathars, Gnosticism, and the "old ways" kept alive under the very nose of an unsuspecting church. Considering the general population of medieval Mediterranean Europe was largely illiterate, pictograms were a useful and necessary way of disseminating information, especially if that information was forbidden folklore. This new compilation, now numbering seventy-eight images, could then have made its way into northern Italy by way of the Marseille/Genoa trade routes during the 1300s and 1400s. If these rough-hewn cards had made their way from Marseille through the Genoa seaports to northern Italy, the decks would have thrived creatively, depicting an early Renaissance Italian society where the cards were not deemed contraband.

Although the Visconti-Sforza family of trionfi cards are considered to be the oldest known Tarot decks in existence today (created in Milan during the mid-1400s), there may be evidence pointing to the contrary. Could it be the earliest known Tarot deck is not the Italian Visconti-Sforza cards but rather a French deck that may date from 1392—the Charles VI deck, also known as the Gringonneur or Estensi deck. The location and date of origin of what is considered to be the most enigmatic of Tarot cards is debated as many place the cards' birth in Venice during the late 1400s. However, there are accounts chronicled in the ledger of the treasurer to King Charles VI of France that specifically record payment to one Jacquemin Gringonneur for three decks of cards created as a distraction to entertain the king. Also, the fashions and costuming worn by the figures depicted in this deck are reminiscent of late fourteenth century French tailoring and dressmaking. It could be considered odd, for if this deck of cards was created for Venetian nobility (a prosperous maritime city-state at the northeastern most border of Italy, on the opposite side of the Marseille trade routes), how could the pack find its way into the estate of an assistant tutor to the grandchildren of Louis XIV? The deck was later bequeathed to the French King in 1711. At the time the Charles VI deck was created, the late medieval era, the city-state of Venice did not appear to engage in established commerce with Mediterranean France. This may be due to the close proximity of Marseille to Venice's fierce competitor, Genoa. Venice primarily utilized the Adriatic, Ionian, and lower Mediterranean seas, the Strait of Gibraltar and the Black Sea for nautical trade. Today, what remains of the Charles VI Tarot deck resides in the Bibliotèque Nationale in Paris consisting of sixteen trump cards plus one court card: the Knave of Swords. Could this be the surviving deck that links the birth of Tarot to thirteenth/fourteenth century France?

In Florence, 1376, a gambling game called *naibbe* was forbidden by decree; the linguistic root for the word "cards" is similar in both Arabic and Spanish: *naib* and *naipes*. Fifteenth-century Italian chronicler Giovanni Covelluzzo reported the game of cards came to the country from the land of the Saracens. Arab Saracens occupied varying portions of the Iberian Peninsula from 710–1491. It is feasible these cards arrived in Italy directly from France by way of the Marseille/Genoa trade routes. Although northern Italy may have enjoyed established trade with al-Andalus during the Caliphate of Cordoba and the ensuing Taifas period of principalities as the Caliphate collapsed, the 1300-1400s would have been a dangerous time for Italian merchant ships to enter the sea-faring channels of the last bastions of Muslim occupied southern Spain as this was a time of constant warfare. Into this mix, stir in the devastating effects of the Black Plague. Arriving on the backs of rats infested with disease-carrying fleas, the deadly malady arrived in Europe from Asia and the Middle East by way of mercantile ships sailing into Genoese ports in 1347. Quickly spreading throughout northern Italy, including Venice and into Mediterranean Europe, maritime trade was crippled during the years of the pandemic (1347–1351, 1361–1362) and the disease's economic effects would be suffered long after. If the Charles VI Tarot deck was to be found in France in 1392 (as many knowledgeable sources would attest), the Black Plague alone—overlooking geography—would appear to have rendered the deck's arrival in French courts from Venice virtually impossible.

Decks in Christian Spain were non-existent; in France the cards would have been few but viable thanks to the craftsmanship of the French Albigensian paper-makers (no coincidence France's neighboring Muslim foes practically invented industrial paper-making). Brutal consequences forced the cards to go underground in Christian Spain and France, the two areas controlled at that time by the rigid fist of the Avignon Papacy. This ecclesiastic period of "papal internment," when the papacy was moved from Rome to France, reigned from 1309 to 1378, successfully surviving the Black Plague. The rarity of the decks that may have been created in France during this period, the cards' indisputable contraband nature, and the inherent peril that accompanied their ownership may be the very reasons no cards from that French century exist today. They simply could not have been cared for nor could the decks flourish as they did in the noble Renaissance courts of northern Italy where Tarot cards were held as a cherished commodity.

It must be taken into consideration that complete Tarot decks did not spontaneously erupt in medieval northern Italy. There is no proven theory as to how, when, or where the twenty-two Major Arcana developed. Some early Italian decks had only fourteen Major Arcana cards and others, like the Minchiate, had an expanded Major Arcana numbering forty-one cards. If one follows the trail from Islamic-held Spain, a logical conclusion could be, because Italy shares no border with Spain, the cards may have gone from northeastern al-Andalus to southwestern France (Marseille) to Italy (Genoa, Milan). Marseille is in immediate proximity to the Genoese seaports. The ports of the southern Iberian Taifas pricipalities with which Genoa had established trade routes would have been a dangerous circumvention of the war-ravaged Islamic Iberian Peninsula during the late 1300s through the 1400s… the approximate time period the Tarot made its appearance in northern Italy. The simplest solution is most often correct.

Chapter Two

Within These Hallowed Halls

The Tarot shares links with secret societies both past and present. Common threads found among esoteric societies are that of freethinking and spiritual mysticism, philosophies frowned upon by cultures of Western antiquity. Fraternities found it necessary to maintain a concealed status. Tarot's first emergence as a hermetic vehicle was developed by a Freemason, Antoine Court de Gébelin (1719–1784). Gébelin was also a member of the Nine Sisters Lodge named for the nine muses of Greek mythology. The lodge was a French fraternity founded in 1771 whose philosophy helped influence the French Revolution of 1789. When one recognizes the close proximity of the American and French Revolutions, it comes as no surprise Freemason Benjamin Franklin became the Venerable Master of the Nine Sisters Lodge in 1777. In 1778, Franklin was given the honor of assisting an eighty-three-year-old Voltaire during the philosopher's initiation into the lodge. François-Marie Arouet (1694–1778), better known as "Voltaire," was a French Enlightenment writer, historian, and philosopher famous for his wit, his attacks on the Catholic church, and his support of freedom of expression. He was an advocate of separation of church and state and embraced religious tolerance, values which paralleled the ideology embraced by the Nine Sisters Lodge, and not surprisingly, the Priory of Sion.

During his initiation, octogenarian Voltaire was supported on his right side by Benjamin Franklin and balanced on his left by Antoine Court de Gébelin, the father of the modern esoteric Tarot. The great Voltaire passed away later that year in May at his home in Paris.

Gébelin was influenced by Italian alchemist and healer Giuseppe Balsamo (1743–1795), otherwise known as the self-styled "Count of Cagliostro"—Master Mason and founder of "Egyptian" Freemasonry (popular in France and Germany in the late 1700s). Balsamo was integral to the adaption of the Egyptian mysteries as applied to the Tarot, as exemplified by the two early French Tarotists, Gébelin and Etteilla (Jean-Baptiste Alliette, 1738–1791) and later by French Martinist Papus (Gerard Encausse 1865–1916). Gébelin penned an essay included in his compendium *The Primeval World, Analyzed and Compared to the Modern World*, volume viii, 1781. This essay was incorporated within a chapter on the Tarot with which his name is forever associated. It was Gébelin's belief the cards held secrets of the ancient Egyptian mystery schools. Writing without the assistance of Egyptian translation or any historical evidence, Gébelin developed a reconstruction of the continental Tarot. He determined Egyptian priests had interpreted the ancient *Book of Thoth* into the Tarot icons. The hermetician declared the images were then brought to Rome where they were held in secrecy by the popes and brought to Avignon during the French papacy. According to Gébelin, it was in this manner the Major Arcana sequence was introduced into France. An essay by Comte de Mellet included in *Monde primitif* gave suggestions for cartomancy; within two years the fortune-teller known as "Etteilla" published a technique for construing the Tarot as a prognosticative oracle and the practice of tarot reading was born.

Other fraternity members figure in key roles within this fascinating drama that is Tarot history. Frenchman, Rosicrucian, and former Freemason Alphonse Louis Constant (1810–1875) was originally a deacon of the Catholic church. Monsieur Constant wrote under the pseudonym Eliphas Levi, which he claimed was a Hebrew translation of his given name. Levi's contributions to the Tarot are substantial, his hermetic tomes copious, and his influence remains a cornerstone of the Tarot community today. He defined the mystical magician and established the links between Cabala, the Hebrew alphabet, and astrology to the continental Tarot deck. His hermetic concepts contained mathematical ideas similar to those of Pythagoras whom he admired.

An avid student of Levi was another noteworthy Parisian, Gerard Encausse (Papus). He helped shape esoteric Tarot with the Egyptian underpinnings popular at the time. The founder of modern Martinism (fraternal lodges steeped in mystical Christianity), Papus was a doctor, philosopher, Theosophist, and alchemist. Papus is known for his definitive work *The Tarot of the Bohemians* and his application of numerology to the Tarot as well as the Cabalistic Tetragrammaton (YHVH, the unpronounceable name of G*d in Judaism).

French occultism was destined to cross the English Chanel to the shores of Victorian Britain where French hermeticians found their equal within the English lodges of Freemasonry and The Golden Dawn. The Hermetic Order of the Golden Dawn was founded in 1886 by three former Freemasons: William Robert Woodman, Samuel Liddell MacGregor Mathers, and William Wynn Westcott. The Order adopted divinatory Tarot as its own and applied its own interpretation to the pack, which has had a major impact on Tarot in English-speaking countries that continues to present day. Most noticeably, the Golden Dawn founders eventually "adjusted" the Major Arcana to more comfortably coincide with the zodiac and Freemasonic philosophy. The original positions of Justice VIII and Strength XI were switched, placing Strength in the eighth position and Justice in the eleventh. The Fool was assigned a value number of 0 and moved from its twentieth or twenty-second position to the first position at the beginning of the deck. The Fool's Hebraic correspondence of Shin or Tav was altered to Aleph, which in turn changed the entire sequence of the allotted Hebrew letters originally assigned to the cards by French occultists. It is a bit odd that The Fool should be assigned Aleph. The Hebrew letter "aleph" has the numerical value of 1 and the card assigned that designation is The Magician. Therefore, assigning Aleph to a valueless or 0 valued card could be considered incorrect or at least inconsistent. Many say the Marseille Tarot remains closest to "the truth," whatever that may be. Today's Tarot varieties and interpretations are left entirely up to individual tastes and beliefs. However, it is my opinion the original Tarots were never intended as a divinatory oracle, rather the pictograms that began as an Arabic card game evolved into a clandestine, camouflaged heretical catechism, elucidating traditions of the suppressed mystical and historical "old ways" that became utterly obliterated and forbidden by a brutal and oppressive Mother Church.

Arthur Edward Waite (1857–1942), the famous British esoteric scholar, was originally born in the United States. He moved from New York to England at an early age when his father died and his mother decided to return to her native England. Waite is the co-creator of what could possibly be the most influential Tarot deck of modern times. Waite joined the Hermetic Order of the Golden Dawn in 1881 but became disenchanted with the group and its direction, defecting to the Freemasons in 1901. Working with artist and fellow Golden Dawn member, Pamela Coleman-Smith, Waite created a rectified Tarot deck featuring scenery on all seventy-eight cards. Waite inserted the Arabic number "0" onto the Fool card, which is discordant within a sequence of otherwise Roman numerated cards. Prior to this, the Minor Arcana were largely "unillustrated," comprised of suit symbols arranged in a specific pattern. Waite's deck was published in 1910 in London by the Rider Company under the title *Tarot Cards* and became known as the *Rider-Waite Deck*. Pamela Coleman-Smith has been recognized for her splendid and iconic artwork only recently; therefore, this seminal deck is now referred to properly as the *Rider-Waite-Smith Deck* or simply as the *RWS*.

No study of continental and Victorian occultism and the Tarot would be complete without mention of the self-proclaimed "wickedest man alive" and although he has been dead for many years, his celebrity lives on in occult studies, poetry, and pop culture—introducing the notorious Aleister Crowley (1875–1947). The self-proclaimed Great Beast was born Edward Alexander Crowley in Warwickshire, England, and grew to become an accomplished chess player, mountaineer, world traveler, novelist, playwright, poet, and avowed hedonist. A highly influential ceremonial magician and former member of the Golden Dawn and Ordo Templi Orientis, Crowley founded the occult philosophy of Thelema. Although his antics are scandalous and legendary, his contributions to Tarot cannot be denied. Crowley joined with artist Lady Frieda Harris to create a unique and powerful Tarot deck. Named the *Thoth Tarot*, after his *Book of Thoth*, the deck is rich in symbolism combined with many divergent disciplines. Sadly, neither Crowley nor Harris would live to see their Tarot concepts in print. Their deck was published in 1969, republished in 1977, further updated in 1986, and continues to be reissued. While not as pervasive as the Waite-Smith deck, the *Thoth Tarot* is essential in the study of divinatory and introspective Tarot.

North America is not without its turn-of-the-century occultists. Paul Foster Case (1888–1954) founded the Masonic-type society "Builders of the Adytum," a Western mystery school that continues to endure. According to Case, eleventh-century philosophers designed the Tarot to both preserve knowledge contained within the incinerated Alexandrian libraries and furnish a universal language. The Tarot deck created by Case appears to be based on the work created by Oswald Wirth, a prominent Swiss occultist affiliated with Papus and Levi; the B.O.T.A. Tarot deck is published uncolored, that task bestowed upon the deck owner.

Manly P. Hall (1901–1990) was a brilliant and prolific author as well as a Mason of the Scottish Rite, achieving this highest of Masonic honors, the 33rd degree, in 1973. The Canadian-born Hall founded The Philosophical Research Society in Los Angeles, California in 1934. This esoteric foundation remains a vibrant study center for students of the Western mysteries world-over. Hall completed his epic *The Secret Teachings of All Ages* (vividly illustrated by J. Augustus Knapp) the same year he achieved the Scottish Rite. Hall joined with Knapp once again to create the enigmatic *Knapp-Hall Tarot*, today a highly collectible deck bursting with unusual symbolism. The pip cards, although modeled after the continental Minors, border on the mysterious and are quite atypical of traditional Tarot offerings.

The Knights Flee

The similarities between the Minor Arcana and today's playing cards are obvious as one is the direct progenitor of the other. Upon closer inspection, one finds an evident difference—the knights are missing from the modern deck's court cards. Instead of fifty-six cards, today's decks number fifty-two. Where did these knights gallop off to?

An assumption exists concerning the cavaliers' removal: the knights' disappearance from playing cards began approximately during the fifteenth century and may have been associated with the downfall of the order. The

Knights Templar were an extraordinary presence during their existence spanning the twelfth to fourteenth centuries. Their influence and contributions to architecture and societal infrastructure have withstood the test of time and are integral to everyday life in modern culture.

It has been suggested besides accumulating astonishing wealth, the Knights were in possession of certain artifacts and parchments plundered from underneath the temple ruins during their original crusades to the holy land in early twelfth century. This cache supposedly supported the heretical tenets that had gone underground and yet were stubbornly prevalent throughout medieval Europe. The church vehemently decried these sacrilegious beliefs as they threatened the very power and stature of the thousand-year-old theocracy. Did the Knights use their discovery as leverage; was this the source of the warrior monks' sudden prosperity? As the order evolved into a lending machine, many monarchs found themselves beholden to the Templars. This situation became volatile in 1307. King Philip IV of France, whose request for membership into the order had been denied, was deeply indebted to the Knights. The sovereign felt the only way to eradicate his debt was to dismantle the order permanently. As the organization had been endorsed by the Catholic Church in 1129, Philip the Fair needed the sanction of the papacy in order to carry out his reprehensible strategy. Procuring consent proved effortless as Mother Church had her own issues with the Templars. The French king conspired with Pope Clement V in 1307 and on Friday October 13, a papal bull was issued and the Knights were arrested *en masse*. Those captured were tortured into giving false confessions and eventually roasted alive at the stake and on spits. Christian monarchs of Europe were ordered to seize all Templar assets—most convenient for the church and indebted kings. Of particular interest our superstition of Friday the 13th may be derived from the Templars' arrest date and it may be no coincidence the fourth Tarot Trump is The Emperor and the fifth Trump is The Pope (Hierophant): Philip IV, Pope Clement V.

The eradication of the Knights was swift and rancorous, but total annihilation proved elusive as many escaped to the shores of Scotland and Portugal in Templar vessels hidden along the French coast. It is this fact that kindles legends of the Templars as there is significant mystery surrounding this move, what they might have taken with them, and what they may have evolved into. Many surviving Knights joined forces with Scotland against England. As King Henry VIII took the throne of England (1491), the image of knights has begun to be excluded from the decks of playing cards in Europe. It would seem probable the knights would remain in an expanded version of playing cards that had branched off from its gaming predecessor, following a more esoteric path. These ensuing decks were published with the adjoining trumps, the mysterious Majors, and these decks of cards would later be infamously utilized in an occult manner.

One facet of the cards needs to be appreciated: besides the cards' historic birth as a gambling game, esoteric Tarot began as an artistic cryptic transmission of forbidden knowledge during a time when one met his or her torturous demise if personal beliefs contradicted church dogma. The same allegory is illustrated in classic religious artwork of the time, especially if originally commissioned by the church. Esoteric Tarot is a very specific thing, a two-part structure—a Major and Minor Arcana, which together totals 78 cards and encompasses the full spectrum of correspondences associated with Western hermeticism, such as Cabala, astrology, alchemy, and numerology. Esoteric Tarot is a standing testament, a sacred text representing the historic timeline from which the cards emerged, the ageless images born of blood and revolution which have metamorphosed, shape-shifting through the centuries. Esoteric Tarot is a synchronistic scroll of language opened for study, offering the privilege of interpretation and glimpses into a forgotten past.

Chapter Three

The Cards

The Pip Cards

The numbered cards or pips comprise forty cards out of the traditional seventy-eight of the modern Tarot deck, ten cards (ace through ten) per each of the four suits. Together with the sixteen court cards (four court cards per suit), they form the Minor Arcana. The traditional pip symbolism utilized in continental Tarot are typically Cups/Chalices, Disks/Coins, Batons/Scepters, and Epees/Swords. Victorian Tarot imagery developed into Cups, Pentacles, Wands, and Swords. The four Tarot suits are each associated with one of the four ancient alchemical elements:

CONTINENTAL	VICTORIAN	MODERN POKER	ELEMENT
Cups/Chalices	Cups	Hearts	Water
Disks/Coins	Pentacles	Diamonds	Earth
Batons/Scepters	Wands	Clubs	Fire
Epees/Swords	Swords	Spades	Air

Each element is associated with its own metaphysical characteristics based on the ancient Neoplatonic universal truths developed by classical Greek philosophers. The alchemical Four Humors have been directly linked to the Tarot since the seventeenth century, and very possibly since before the Renaissance.

ELEMENT/DIR.	ATTRIBUTE	ETHEREAL ATTRIBUTE	HUMOR	QUALITY	SEASON
Water/s.	Emotion	Spirituality	Phlegmatic	cold/wet	Winter
Earth/w.	Assets	Fertility	Melancholic	cold/dry	Autumn
Fire/n.	Production	Creativity	Choleric	hot/dry	Summer
Air/e.	Ethics	Intellect	Sanguine	hot/wet	Spring

The Neoplatonic Four Humors' presentation of the four seasons is quite eloquent. Tarot was born of Western esotericism and, when interpreting its correspondences, it must be from that point of reference. Wands' seasonal attribution of Summer is apparent in its alchemical element of Fire: the hottest time of year is linked with the hottest element. Because life is based on the balance of opposites, the suit of Wands is balanced by its polar opposite Cups, whose element is Water, the alchemical opposite of Fire. Cups' seasonal correspondence would then be the polar opposite of Summer, which is Winter. This also makes sense as winter is the season in the Western world in which water can appear in all its myriad forms: vapor, rain, ice, sleet, snow etc. It is apparent the two extreme seasons, summer and winter, are polar opposites. That leaves the two remaining medial seasons: the opposing seasons of fall and spring. The elements of Earth and Air are also polar opposites: material and non-material. The suit of Disks represents Earth and fertility; at no time of year does earth give forth more of her riches than at autumn harvest, placing Disks where it belongs in Autumn. The opposite of harvesting is planting; planting is done in springtime. This seats the suit of Swords in Spring. Traditional, ancient sacrificial blood-letting, the act of spilling animal blood in order to fertilize the ground and appease the gods, was done in spring. In order to sacrifice an animal, a ceremonial blade was necessary. Of particular interest is the holy day, Easter. The celebration of the risen sacrificial lamb is associated with the Vernal Equinox. The actual name *Easter* originates from the pagan celebration of earth's springtime renewal, Ostara, and goddess Eostre.

The four suits are said to represent the mundane experience of mankind. Upon examining the pips further, it is found they are actually in possession of very definite "personalities" which, not surprisingly, encompass the spectrum of the human experience.

Cups—feminine—Winter

Often associated with love, romance, and marriage, the suit of Cups also represents the higher aspirations of spirituality and emotional evolution. Just as its element Water flows and ebbs, so do the moods contained within this suit. As water can be very tumultuous, the suit of Cups can indeed be a wild ride. As water fills up and takes the shape of its container so the suit of Cups exemplifies adaptability. The inward energy of this suit is associated with the feminine principle of Yin in Chinese philosophy and its symbol typifies the Grail Cup.

Disks—feminine—Autumn

Possessions, security, and fertility are interwoven with nature in this lush suit. The relationships of body and balance are personified by the suit of Disks, as is procuring health, wealth, and happiness. Humankind's correlation with its surrounding environment underlies the importance of material success within this world, success achieved by the exchange of goods and services, wise investments, and achieving a successful harvest. The energy of this suit is associated with Mother Earth and its symbol, the circle, represents the continuing cycle of life.

Wands—Male—Summer

Fiery Wands are the suit of action, confidence, creativity, adventure, and a zest for life. The suit of Wands stokes the fires of industry and represents the ambition and drive that is required to keep those fires burning. Chinese philosophy lends the male principle of Yang to the outward energy of this suit, and its symbol represents the scepters specifically crowned by the iconic fleur-de-lis (later stylized as "clubs" in modern playing cards) which, bedecked in precious metals and jewels, adorned the tops of royal staves wielded by the regal hands of Europe.

Swords—Male—Spring

On the higher ethereal plane, the suit of Swords encompasses all intellectual concerns including thought, reason, truth, justice, and ethical principles. However, when and wherever intellect is involved, one shall find the foundations of ego at work as well resulting in situations that could be problematic to varying degrees. The energy of this suit is associated with the ether, which provides the medium for evolved intellect and the suit symbol represents the wisdom of humankind in motion through the ages. Taken in context, this suit's presence may be troubling.

The Court Cards

The Tarot court is comprised of sixteen cards that make up the Royal Arcana. Together with the forty pips, they complete the fifty-six cards of Tarot's Minor Arcana. Traditionally, each of the four suits is inhabited by four occupants of the royal feudal court; they reside at the end of each suit sequence. These cards are commonly known and sequenced as Page, Knight, Queen, and King. Depending on a deck's theme, these titles and sequences can change; some of these examples are specific methods of maintaining the gender neutrality of the Tarot court as the Queen is usually the only female member of the hierarchy. In *The Illuminati Tarot: Keys of Secret Societies*, the royals are attributed grades in ascending order: Novice, Initiate, Adept, and Magus. Not only does this illustrate the initiatory nature of esoteric fraternities, but also the maturation of the human psyche within the Royals and their distinct suit element.

When using Tarot for divinatory purposes, the Royal Arcana often signify actual people (the self, or others past, present, or future) that embody the personality of their suit. However, these cards are complex as the human personality is composed of innumerable variables. The court members are ascribed the attributes of the four basic alchemical elements:

Kings (Magi)—Fire, indicating the primary overt masculine dynamic of prominence, dominance, authority, order, judgment, and strategy. Personage: approximately age thirty-five or older, father figure, authority figure, wisdom, and experience

Queens (Adepts)—Water, indicating the primary subtle feminine dynamic of love, beautification, support, presence, intuition, reassurance, and knowledge. Personage: approximately age thirty-five or older, mother figure, authority figure, maturity, nurturing, and understanding.

Knights (Initiates)—Air, indicating the secondary masculine dynamic of forward motion, action, strength, courage, law, drive, and instinct. Personage: approximately age twenty to thirty-five, male or female, metamorphosis, maturation, adventure, and risk taking.

Page (Novices)—Earth, indicating the secondary female dynamic of creativity, sensitivity, devotion, amenity, and meditation. Personage: possibly son or daughter, approximately age infant to nineteen, male or female, the messengers, playful children, pleasure, and spontaneity.

Each of the four nobles embodies one of the four Hebrew letters of the Tetragrammaton, the unpronounceable name of the Hebrew G*d. The Tetragrammaton יהוה is comprised of the letters Yod, Heh, Vav, Heh (traditionally read from right to left in Hebrew) and is integral to the Jewish mystical system of Cabala. This arrangement of letters can be transliterated as Jehovah or Yahweh: J/Y=Yod, H=Heh, V/W=Vav, and H=Heh.

The Court is assigned these Tetragrammaton designations:

Kings: Yod י
Queens: Heh ה
Knights: Vav ו
Knaves: Heh ה

The Court cards possess different authority. The Page's position differs from, but is not inferior to, that of the Knight, Queen, and King. Neither court card is no less important than the other but there are different levels of suit maturity represented by the succession of status: the Wands Court—the Page (Novice) ignites the flame, the movement of the Knight (Initiate) is the required combustion, the nature of the Queen (Adept) represents the nurturing of the flame, and the King (Magus) gives the resulting illumination. When the status and suit elements are identical, that court persona is the purest demonstration of the suit: Magus of Wands (Fire of Fire), Adept of Cups (Water of Water), Initiate of Swords (Air of Air), and Novice of Disks (Earth of Earth). The nature of a suit may work against the quality of court card in a reading. Surrounding and dignifying cards in a Tarot spread help to clarify this.

Novices are the seedling expressions of the suit characteristics. They represent the sparks of ideas. They are too immature to possess an astrological quality; they embody the suit element at its most rudimentary and are prone to caprice. There is no inherent threat rooted in the four Novice court cards but there exists a lack of boundaries. The Novices are naturally intuitive and talkative thus the quintessential messengers of the Tarot deck. If there is a communication to be delivered, these couriers are at the ready!

Initiates represent the maturation process; suit dynamics are beginning to develop. Initiates adventure in order to achieve their objectives and discover a sense of self. The cavaliers seek out life's challenges, translating these experiences into life lessons. Initiates often quest in service to others, their own agenda becomes secondary. This quality becomes intrinsic to the personal growth indigenous to the four horsemen of the Court. Initiates are emissaries as well, although their deliveries tend to be of a more serious nature than Novices' communiqués.

Adepts bring to their suit a motherly wisdom. They motivate rather than dictate and inspire rather than perspire. These ladies bring to their suit refinement and beauty, knowledge and intuition. Adepts are very powerful and fiercely protective as the Queens of the esoteric game of chess demonstrate. They are matriarchs of the suits and can enforce their will and authority. These noblewomen tend to be unrepentant in their governance; however, their actions are grounded in poise, encouragement, and love.

Magi embody authority and imbue their suits with patriarchal sensibility and wisdom that can only be cultivated by maturity and experience. Magi make sound decisions regarding the welfare of not only their families, but of others as well. The monarchs of the Tarot court accept this great responsibility without hesitation and instill order and control through personality and strategy. These sovereigns bring qualities and elemental attributes of the suits to culmination, realization, and fulfillment.

The Major Arcana

The fifth suit of the Tarot deck is the Major Arcana, or the trump cards, as historically their value was highest in medieval trick-taking games. The traditional sequence consists of twenty-one titled and numbered cards plus an un-numbered or zero valued Fool card. The Majors have developed into the crux of the Tarot: the trumps can stand apart from the Minors as many Tarot decks are comprised of just the twenty-two Majors. However, one will not find a complete Tarot deck consisting of only pip and court cards, interesting when one takes into consideration Tarot began as a suited card game devoid of a Major Arcana. There are interpretations regarding the origins, meanings, appearance, and sequential order of the trumps thus affecting the associated minors. Schools of thought impacting modern Tarot trumps find their origins specifically in Spain, France, and Italy.

The earliest continental Tarots were based on the Gra/Ari-Gra version of the Sephir Yetzirah and Alexandrian hermeticism. The Sephir Yetzirah is an ancient Jewish creation manuscript of which there are several accounts. There are four primary versions of the Sephir Yetzirah: Saadia's, the Short and Long (ninth/tenth century), and the (Ari) Gra, a late eighteenth-century digest which many consider to be the correct version. This version was developed by Eliyahu, the Gaon of Vilna, known as the "Gra." He published his Sephir Yetzirah during the late 1700's based on the Ari's (Rabbi Isaac Luria) interpretations a hundred years prior. Both are redacted versions of the Short version complementing the text with the Zohar, the foundational collection of books containing mystical Cabala. The Ari-Gra version has been most popular in Hasidic circles and Western esoteric movements.

These early continental decks evolved into the French versions presented by occultists such as Etteilla (1700s) and Levi, Wirth, Picard, and Papus during the mid-to-late 1800s. Christian heresies such as astrology, numerology, Cabala, and Gnosticism were integral to the development of these later French Tarots. These paradigms eventually crossed the channel to the shores of Britain where the Victorian/Edwardian lodges adopted and adapted the Tarot as their own. Prime examples of these hermetics would be the *Rider-Waite-Smith Tarot* and, decades later, the *Golden Dawn*/Crowley/*Thoth* decks. Today, the British system of Tarot is most prevalent in English speaking countries where the RWS deck and its myriad of clones reign supreme, followed by Crowley's Thoth and Golden Dawn decks. However, the questions remain: where did the trump cards come from, when did they first appear, and when did they join the Minor Arcana?

Some say the Major Arcana represent the karmic journey of the soul (Cabala, Hinduism, Buddhism), or the travails of Parcival (Holy Grail), while others claim the trumps were created as a literal flash card system conveying the tenets of clandestine Christian heresy (Gnosticism). A deck produced in medieval Florence in the 1400s consisted of Majors numbering forty to forty-two trumps. This expanded arcana included the twelve signs of the zodiac, the four alchemical elements, and the four cardinal virtues. This deck was originally created for the card game Minchiate and is associated with that name. Approximately eighteen cards of the Minchiate Majors correspond to traditional Tarot trumps and it is this type of deck that lends credence to the theory the Major Arcana may have begun as an educational tool.

The prevailing theory states Tarot had its beginnings as Tarocchi in early fifteenth century northern Italy and was subsequently introduced into southern France when the French conquered Milan and the Piedmont in 1499. If true, the precursors of the seminal Tarot de Marseille would have been introduced into southern France at approximately that time. Although the Italian Visconti-Sforza trionfi decks are considered to be the oldest known Tarot decks created during the mid-1400s, there could be evidence pointing to 1300s France as Tarot's genesis and its melding of the Major and Minor Arcana. The date of origin of the Tarot de Marseille is debated; it is proclaimed the deck had been created as early as the 1200s or as late as the 1600s—a 400-year discrepancy!

There exists a theory the Major Arcana were devised in medieval northern Italy as an expansion for existing decks. These were based on Christian traditions and feudal society. It is unknown how many images comprised these early trumps as extant examples in museums and private collections are incomplete. The Italian prototypes were created by Italian artists in and around Tuscany and Lombardy beginning in the 1400s. The cards were unnumbered, untitled, and varied in sequence. However, the immediate proximity of Muslim-occupied Spain to France and the birth of Gothic architecture (Arab in origin) in this same region gives rise to notions which counter the traditional Italian source of Tarot.

Who Drew the Twenty-Two?

During the period early European decks began circulating one could die a torturous death if one's beliefs contradicted church dogma. Could these miniature pictograms employed in games of chance and gambling have also doubled as a clandestine flash card system, a way of keeping the "old ways"—astrology, numerology, Judaic mysticism, and Christian heresy—alive in plain view under the nose of ruling theocracy? Is that why the church outlawed these cards and their related games?

Once again there are many theories and not enough space here to discuss them all. Another aspect of the Tarot must be addressed, for it is this feature of the deck structure that evolves fifty-six medieval heraldic images into the most infamous and mystical of all oracles. This is the inscrutable fifth suit of the Tarot: the twenty-two trumps—the Major Arcana. It is widely believed the Majors depict the soul's archetypal karmic journey through this life and the next. Perhaps the trumps were added to the original Minors not only as an added facet to a game of chance but also as a heretical informational tool, a way of communicating the teachings and history of a millennium past, suppressed by the theocratic regime.

Most theories place the birth of the trump cards in the noble courts of Renaissance Italy. Author Ronald Decker has researched this notion to great extent. In his book *The Esoteric Tarot: Ancient Sources Rediscovered in Hermeticism and Cabala* , Mr. Decker has arrived at an exact date the first trumps combined with the minor arcana appeared: 1441. The author surmised, through his investigations, the trumps were commissioned by the court of Ferrara as an honorarium for a young visitor, Milanese princess Bianca Maria (1424–1468). But, Mr. Decker believes the request came from the princess. Therefore, according to Mr. Decker's theory (which is greatly over-simplified here), the trumps were a creation of one of two noble Italian courts—Milan or Ferrara.

Did the Major Arcana ever exist as their own entity independent of the Minors? Theories maintain trump prototypes are found among late medieval instructive cards used as visual aids for memorization typically religious in nature. These systems of colorful images were utilized at a time when books and Bibles were expensive and rare, seldom seen in medieval society. These cards depicted saints, their symbols, biblical and mythological characters, cardinal sins and virtues, the seven known planets, the signs of the zodiac, and other data relevant to those denizens of early Renaissance society.

In The Grail Procession, author Justin E. Griffin agrees with author, Grail scholar, and researcher Margaret Starbird and Tarot experts Paul Huson and Amber Jayanti:

> The first apparent Tarot deck was created in 1393 by the painter Charles Gringonneur, allegedly to placate the mentally ill King Charles VI of France. Now only a portion of this deck remains intact. In the Bibliotèque du Roi in Paris, one can still see the Fool, Emperor, Pope, Lovers, Wheel of Fortune, Temperance, Fortitude, Justice, Moon, Sun, Chariot, Hermit, Hanged Man, Death, Tower and Last Judgment cards . . . *The Grail Procession* (Justin E. Griffin, McFarland & Co., 2004) Note: Mr. Griffin has misidentified Monsieur Gringonneur, whose first name was Jacquemin, not Charles.

This school of thought places the oldest known Tarot deck in France, preceding the Visconti-Sforza of northern Italy by half a century. These Italian variants are thought to be the oldest extant decks by most Tarot historians but accepted history always has underlying disparities. Could it be the earliest known Tarot deck in existence is not of the Italian family of cards but rather the deck dating from 1393 France—the Charles VI deck, also known as the Gringonneur deck? The origin and date of these cards is debated as some place the cards in late 1400s Venice. However, there are accounts recorded in the treasurer's ledger of Charles VI of France that specifically record payment in 1392 to one Jacquemin Gringonneur for three decks of cards to entertain the king. Also, the fashions of the depicted figures are reminiscent of fourteenth century French haute couture. If this deck was created in Italy, why then should it be included in the estate of an assistant tutor to the grandchildren of French king Louis XIV, and later bequeathed to the king's eldest son in 1711? The deck now resides in the Bibliotèque Nationale (*Bibliotèque du Roi*) in Paris consisting of sixteen trump cards plus one court card. Could this be the surviving deck that links the birth of Tarot to France?

It is important to remember Muslim playing cards contained no Major Arcana; they were comprised of forty pip cards and twelve to sixteen court cards, which probably did not include queens. At least one of the decks painted for King Charles in 1392 contained both the Minor and Major Arcana. If the Charles VI/Gringonneur deck is truly the earliest extant Tarot deck, it can be surmised the Major Arcana was first created in France where it was combined with existing decks of suited gaming cards…but, created by whom and why? Should one look to the Gothic cathedrals of France and the ruthless suppression by the medieval church for answers?

The Majors of the Gringonneur deck have familiar themes, however, their appearance is strikingly different from traditional trumps. Their artistic aesthetics suggest they may have been based on earlier, simpler images that possessed hidden meaning. As the Arabic playing cards had no Major Arcana, it is plausible the Major Arcana was devised in France where perhaps the pictograms existed separately from the playing cards as their own iconic teaching tool, a visual catechism of Gnosticism and heretical teachings.

Preceding the Gringonneur deck by sixty-three years, the French text, *Le Folie Perceval* (1330), retells the story of the quest for the Holy Grail. What makes this tale so remarkable is the manner in which the manuscript relates the travails and triumphs of Parcival . . . it mimics the Major Arcana and its sequence! It is not unreasonable to conclude the author was intentional in the presentation of the four grail hallows: the Lance, Chalice, Sword, and Dish (Wands, Cups, Swords, and Pentacles). The hallows were the spear that pierced Christ's side, the cup from which he drank at the last supper, the bowl that caught his blood during the Crucifixion, and the sword that beheaded John the Baptist. Who may have been in possession of these artifacts? It is established the Cathars had a cooperative alliance with the Knights Templar. It is presumed these First Crusaders discovered an assortment of religiously significant treasure, relics, and documents when excavating the ruins of Solomon's Temple in Jerusalem (1096-99) and fought alongside the Cathars during the siege of Montségur (1244). Legend maintains five survivors of the battle escaped with a mysterious cache.

Many of the genre believe the twenty-two images of the Major Arcana were originally created by Cathars, a peaceable gnostic French society (1143–1325) which was perceived to be very counter-productive to church objectives. The Cathars were renowned for their papermaking craftsmanship. Tarot is rooted in Neoplatonic philosophy and scholarly efforts indicating the

French Cathar influence on Tarot are presently being published. There exists an excellent article by Dr. Robert V. O'Neill, *Neo-Platonism and the Tarot*, at Tarot.com. In his landmark study of the Major Arcana's historic and esoteric foundations, *Tarot Symbolism* (1986), Dr. O'Neill has detailed Tarot's emergence along with its philosophical and metaphysical underpinnings to the ancient teachings of Plato and Neoplatonism, Gnosticism, Cabala, alchemy, medieval memory arts, numerology, and astrology. Dr. O'Neill's current work includes an examination of the contribution by the medieval heresy of Catharism on the Tarot and recently Robert Swiryn has published *The Secret of the Tarot: How the Story of the Cathars Was Concealed in the Tarot of Marseilles*.

There is yet another twist in the Royal Road. Abbot Suger (1081–1151) was a Frankish abbot, statesman, and father of Gothic architecture who lived during the early period of the Cathar movement. The Gothic cathedrals are astounding libraries of ancient knowledge chiseled in stone, incorporated with magnificent glasswork utilizing light and darkness to recount mystical legends, metaphors, riddles, and labyrinths. Suger was the abbot of St. Denis, which was founded in the seventh century by Merovingian Dagobert I and rebuilt by Suger. Contrary to the restrictive dogma of his Catholicism, the Benedictine clergyman was influenced by Dionysius' Gnostic theology of light, Christian esotericism, the bloom of Catharism, and Neoplatonism. It is also rumored this architectural genius created a rudimentary version of the twenty-two Major Arcana.

Neoplatonism and Gnostic theosophy was infused into the medieval construction of European Gothic cathedrals, churches, and chapels. According to Dr. Robert V. O'Neill, the architectural style developed by Suger "was encyclopedic, hierarchical, symbolic, and cosmic in dimension." Suger brought within the cold dark walls of sanctity a liturgical experience that was radiant, mystical, and spiritually inspiring. By employing stained-glass techniques created by Arab artisans and architectural designs developed and employed by Arab draftsmen, Suger was able to permeate his designs with a mélange of ever-changing prisms and dancing beams of light.

Not coincidentally, Suger's rebuilding of Saint-Denis Abbey coincided with the arrival of documents and relics brought back to France from Jerusalem by Templar crusaders. Abbot Suger enjoyed a deep friendship with the king of France and was an associate of Bernard de Clairvaux, a church advocate for the Knights Templar. Some say the Cistercian cleric and Abbot Suger were dear friends, others declare they loathed each other. It is possible, through these relationships, Suger had access to these mysterious parchments and artefacts. It is theorized some of these parchments contained genealogies of the Holy Royal Family. It would also be very likely the Knights returned with examples of Arab culture and architecture, as many First Crusaders were Palestinian by birth. Gothic architecture has its roots in Arab structural design and Abbot Suger conceived its European counterpart; it is reasonable to determine Suger was privy to the information and valuables brought back from the first crusades. The Templars themselves became the finest of stonemasons and draftsmen, perpetuating Suger's methods and Gothic designs. It is conceivable Knights also brought back with them the card game so popular with their enemy, the Muslim forces. If this truly occurred, it is not implausible Suger would have been introduced to these small, fascinating paper images utilized for gaming pastimes.

The stone walls of Gothic cathedrals are infamous for their mysterious, very non-Christian depictions of esoteric, hermetic, and pagan traditions; it is thought by some researchers these churches reflect the basic foundations of the Major Arcana. These traditions, often chiseled in an encoded medium, were considered heretical by the church and punishable by brutal measures. Still, carvings of the Green Man, the Jewish Magen David, labyrinths, and the zodiac are but a few of many pagan, esoteric, and hermetic references that adorn the great walls of these magnificent edifices. The designers of these glorious buildings took great chance allowing suppressed traditions to thrive, out of sight to the blind eyes of an unseeing church but easily visible to the initiated. Some say the father of Gothic architecture, towards the end of his life, created an encoded sequence of paper icons in the form of twenty-two pictograms. Why twenty-two images? As a Gnostic well versed in hermetic sciences, Abbot Suger would have been familiar with the twenty-two letters of the Hebrew alphabet, the twenty-two paths of the Cabalistic Tree of Life, and the numerological implications of the number twenty-two—a master number and the number representing the Master Builder, a title Suger could apply to himself or God. Similarly, in Freemasonry, God is referred to as the Grand Architect. As a medieval engineer, Suger would have used 22/7 instead of *pi* in his construction schematic. As a Benedictine monk, Suger would have been thoroughly versed in the twenty-two chapters of the Book of Revelation, a component of the New Testament many believe to be the encrypted Gnostic verses of the Beloved Apostle. Certainly the abbot and his colleague from Clairveaux celebrated the feast day of St. Mary Magdalene, the twenty-second day of July. In the St. Denis scriptorium, the abbot may have inked leaves created by the Albigensian rag paper-making process. Possibly, amid the dynamic and dangerous theological trends of the time, Suger chose to create a system by which the old suppressed ways of mysticism, biblical history, and spirituality could be kept alive. This would have included the acknowledgement that Jesus was fully human, a royal and a rabbi, and completely immersed in the human experience as it pertained to his life, times, and social stature. This would have necessitated marriage and family.

Prized copies of these "flash" cards may have been created, some coming into the possession of the traveling troubadours of southern twelfth century France. These minstrels of music and poetry journeyed throughout France spreading a new philosophy, that of courtly love and the preciousness of the fairer sex, the antithesis of medieval church teachings but reminiscent of Jesus' original teachings. France was witnessing a mysterious trend—the troubadours preached the adoration of women and the ennoblement of man through love. This movement was not to survive. An oppressive church came crashing down in a vicious effort to crush this new way of life. The resulting atrocities include the French Albigensian Crusade beginning in 1184—a twenty year genocide that brutally eradicated much of Cathar society and ultimately led to four hundred merciless years of Catholic Inquisitions.

Hypothetically speaking, in an effort to keep Gnosticism alive, the twenty-two heretical pictograms originally conveyed by Abbot Suger were combined with a benign deck of playing cards popular in France during the thirteenth century. The pictograms may have been cloaked as trump cards, expanding the existing gaming decks by adding an all-powerful fifth suit. This new trump-taking game would naturally have crossed the borders back into Spain and eventually Italy. Though these decks were eventually outlawed by the church in mid-1300, first in Spain and France and eventually several areas in northern Italy, the decks managed to survive. The simple fact the Italian cards first emerged in northern Italy may illustrate not only the influence of the Italian Renaissance, but the impact of the French/Italian border and the flow of playing cards from Al Andalus, to the redesigned, expanded Tarot decks of France, to the magnificent Italian Tarocchi versions of the Renaissance. Due to the prohibition of the earliest Spanish and French decks, the cards became contraband, forced to go underground, and none of these decks, if they did indeed exist, are extant today. The French Gringonneur/Charles VI deck is quite possibly the oldest collection in existence—an exquisite, fragile aide-mémoire of Tarot's embattled account, the cards' haunting history before its journey of transformation, becoming that most infamous of oracles, the seventy-eight cards of the Royal Road.

Chapter four

The Priory of Sion

The Mother of Secret Societies

Perhaps author Lionel Fanthorpe says it best when he states "The Priory of Sion may be one of the most ancient, powerful, and remarkable secret societies in the world or it may be the last vestigial trace of an inner group of Knights Templars or it could be a perfectly innocent, respectable, and prosaic friendly society or it may not exist at all."

Mere mention of the shadowy group guarantees to elicit enthusiastic debate. Many global forums dedicated to the study of the Priory foster discussion that often escalates to the point of unpleasantness. The fraternity has its devoted supporters, some quite well known, and its equally committed detractors, some quite infamous. Two films of recent release deal with the Priory of Sion directly—one film a nationally acclaimed blockbuster, the other a provocative, limited-engagement documentary. Cloaks and daggers abound, speculation is tossed about, and outsiders endeavor to become insiders in this mysterious, sometimes sinister world of the Priory of Sion. However, this space is not dedicated to the debate of its existence, whether or not it was the brainchild of a twentieth century Parisian hoaxer or founded by a branch of Templar Knights in the kingdom of Jerusalem. Conclusions are best drawn by individuals and their own research.

The Priory tale cannot be told without relating the founding of the Templar Knights as the two may be a direct result of the other. In 1118, approximately twenty years after the recapture of Jerusalem from Muslim occupation, Hughes de Payen, a vassal of the Count of Champagne and relation by marriage to the St. Clairs (Sinclairs) of Roslin, presented to King Baldwin II of Jerusalem a small group of men. Baldwin II was cousin to Jerusalem's first medieval ruler, Godfrey de Bouillon, who had led first crusaders to victory in the holy land twenty years earlier. The minute militia presented to the king were chevaliers of France who served under Godfrey de Bouillon. As history would relate the tale, this new order of knights committed themselves to the defense of the holy land, providing safe passage for those on pilgrimage and living a life of chastity and austerity. The nine warrior monks were given lodging in a palace wing built upon the Temple Mount, site of the ruined Temple of Solomon, giving the order their name "The Poor Fellow-Soldiers of Christ and of the Temple of Solomon," more commonly known as the Knights Templar. Formally endorsed by the church in 1129, this is the story history prefers to chronicle about these first infamous Templars.

During the ensuing two centuries, the order became among the most wealthy and powerful of the Western Christian military orders and a significant monetary lending machine. The Knights became a favoured charity throughout Europe and grew rapidly in membership and influence. The Templars, sporting distinctive white mantles emblazoned with their iconic red cross, were among the most skilled fighting units of the Crusades. Non-combatant comrades of the order managed a large financial infrastructure, revolutionizing the present day economic systems. The order instituted a fundamentally early form of banking, lending, and credit structures.

There are some events mainstream history does not convey, perhaps because these occurrences do not fit the accepted paradigm. These events require more investigation, perusing pages of accepted truths to find nuggets of information that do not seem to fit properly in the pictures. For the following nine years after the Knights set up camp in the palace of Kings Baldwin I and II, they admitted no new members to their order. That is odd as nine founding members hardly seems an adequate number of sentries to patrol all the byways leading into and out of the holy land. Surprisingly, there is no historical proof these Knights engaged in such activities. It appeared to European powers during those first nine years the order was embedded in Jerusalem the Knights accomplished essentially nothing. William of Tyre (1130–1186), prelate and primary chronicler of the age, mentions the Knights sparingly: he relates in Book 12, chapter 7 that nine years after the order's formation there remained only nine Templars. Had William's silence been required? Did continental sponsors realize the warrior monks had access to tunnels underneath the abandoned Temple stables? It is now known the Knights excavated the Temple Mount during those nine years—was that their original intended mission? Authors speculate when Roman legions destroyed the Temple in 70 CE, they absconded with only obvious loot, unwittingly abandoning the most valuable treasures which may have included the Ark of the Covenant, the artifact perceived to be the holy grail, documents, and genealogies including that of Jesus, his marriage(s) and ensuing issue which may have branched into the Merovingian dynasty. This cache could have been hidden easily by Temple priests in any of the numerous tunnels known to have existed below Temple stables on the Temple Mount. Could this clandestine collection have been the purpose behind the establishment of the order—an operation founded on rediscovering truths passed down from Solomon through the ages? It is no coincidence the central characters integral to the Templars' creation were all of Merovingian descent. This recovered cache of forbidden knowledge could have provided the Knights Templar with unprecedented leverage with both the Mother Church and European royalty.

What exactly is a priory? The American Dictionary states a priory is a religious house governed by a prior or prioress and most times dependent upon an abbey. When Jerusalem fell to victorious crusaders, there existed the ruins of an ancient Byzantine basilica atop a hill looming to the south of Jerusalem. The peak recognized as Mount Sion was home to the "Mother of all Churches," as the ruined basilica had been known. This became the site for a magnificent fortified abbey christened the Abbey de Notre Dame du Mont de Sion, erected by the ruler of Jerusalem, Godfrey de Bouillon. The abbey housed occupants, most likely the knights of the crusade, who possibly developed into a fraternity unto itself, perhaps an autonomous order taking their name from the very site in which they lived…the Order or Priory of Sion which predated the origination of the Knights Templar by approximately twenty years. Of interest is Godfrey de Bouillon and Baldwin I did not earn the reign of Jerusalem through blood, they were elected. Certain documents state Baldwin I owed his throne to the "Order." The documents continue: the Order's official seat was the Abbey of Notre Dame de Sion in Jerusalem.

Priory expert and author Robert Howells says today's Priory of Sion is not only an organization, but an ideal and philosophy as well, and assuredly involved in the machinations of the world both past and present and will be well into the future. Many recent publications have focused public awareness on the bloodline aspects of the Priory, which appear to be its raison d'etre, if not the reason for its founding—the protection of the holy royal bloodline throughout the cen¬turies. However, Mr. Howells states unequivocally that the Priory's scope of activities varies greatly from the occult to Middle Eastern politics. Mr. Howells declares: "The political weight of Sion cannot be underestimated. To achieve its aim of a marriage of Eastern and Western philosophies, it is increasingly involved in Arab-Israeli politics with the intention of putting an end to the infighting among Christians, Muslims, and Jews." One wonders what is this mysterious Priory of Sion, has it really been among us for so long, and how benign (or not) is it? An unanswerable question, for the Priory does not appear to be a group of chaps who enjoy secret handshakes, ambiguous rituals, and expensive scotch. To quote the beginning of chapter 1 of Isaiah 28.16: "I lay in Zion for a foundation of stone, a tried stone, a precious corner stone, a sure foundation."

Chapter Five

The Major Arcana

The Fool

"It is often hard in the case of Plantard to find the line what is known and what is a good story."

—Dan Burstein
Author, *Secrets of the Code* and *Secrets of Mary Magdalene*

Is it possible a seemingly innocuous twentieth century Parisian could be at the epicenter of the biggest religious quake of modern times? Pierre Athanase Marie Plantard (de Saint-Clair) was born March 18, 1920, the son of a butler and a concierge—a mundane birth for someone so illustrious as to be declared to be the twelfth/fifteenth Grand Master of the Priory of Sion (1981 and 1989 according to one of the two alternate lists) and a direct descendant of the Merovingians thus Jesus Christ. Many words have been used to describe the monsieur: huckster, conman, scapegoat, anti-Semite, resistance fighter, spy, counter-spy… the list goes on, but the name Pierre Plantard de Saint-Clair will be forever linked with the Priory of Sion.

Plantard's detractors (of which there are many) allege the Priory of Sion sprung from the Parisian's own political machinations in 1956 when he registered the Prieuré de Sion as an official organization in France. Subsequently, a mysterious set of documents called the *Dossiers Secrets* were surreptitiously deposited in the French National Library by an anonymous donor. These pages contain a collection of esoterica, genealogies, and a list of Grand Masters who had presided over the Priory through the centuries. Several years later, in 1967, the wheels began to turn with the publication of *The Accursed Treasure of Rennes-le-Ch*âteau by a contemporary of Plantard's, Gérard de Sède. This in turn inspired English author and BBC scriptwriter Henry Lincoln who read the book by Sède while on vacation in France. He created a series of documentaries examining the perplexing links between the tiny French village of Rennes-le-Château and the Priory of Sion. A collaboration soon followed between Lincoln and authors Michael Baigent and Richard Leigh and the controversial book that unexpectedly shocked society on a global level was born. The bestseller *Holy Blood, Holy Grail* by Baigent, Lincoln, and Leigh was published in 1982 and continues to be released worldwide in as many languages. The book was the basis for the Ron Howard blockbuster *The Da Vinci Code* (2006). Have all these occurrences been the gears of the Priory rotating according to plan? Or is it all just a simple hoax perpetrated by an enigmatic Parisian gone amazingly awry?

Meaning

Archangel: Lumiel
Cabala: Path 32, Malkuth-Yesod
Element: Fire
Hebrew: Shin

The Fool is typically interpreted as the novice beginning the journey through twenty-two degrees of initiation, symbolic of the soul's karmic journey through life, thereafter, and back again. Many of history's secret fraternities interpreted the trumps as a chronicle of The Fool's mystical indoctrination through the twenty-two doors of the Major Arcana. He is presented in very early continental decks as a hapless court jester harassed by a trio of boys and in some versions it is rather disturbing, almost pedophilic. Many have come to know him as the iconic Victorian happy wanderer. In some decks he is blindfolded, sometimes accompanied by a crocodile, dog, or cat any of which may or may not be pestering him.

The Fool is the only trump to inhabit three different positions in the traditional Majors' sequence, the designation being related to the deck's esoteric philosophy. The standard continental decks gave The Fool no numerical value and placed the card toward the end of the Major Arcana designated Shin after Judgment XX and before The World XXI, or Tav as the final card in the sequence after The World XXI (as the final card The Fool sometimes had no Hebraic designation). In the final position, The Fool appears to have completed his karmic journey; however, inserting The Fool between Judgment and The World places more responsibility on this carefree spirit; he may proceed towards enlightenment or make bad choices causing him to fall back to the beginning of the deck. The Victorian fraternities took a different approach, assigning The Fool Aleph and an Arabic value of '0' and placing him at the beginning of a Major Arcana designated with Roman numerals. This re-positioning of The Fool changes the original Hebraic and astrological correspondences as well as meanings of the cards. However, all of these arrangements are easily interpreted as The Fool's karmic journey: about to embark on his quest, at karmic crossroads, or realizing karmic completion.

As the trump's element Fire is erratic, so is the nature of The Fool; he embodies youthful enthusiasm. However, this thirst for experience is accompanied by impulsiveness. The Cabbalistic path of Hod–Malkuth is that of Perpetual Intelligence, The Fool's elusive objective.

Keywords

Spontaneity, freedom, possibility, optimism. Options, choices. Joy of adventure, opportunities both negative and positive. Restlessness, infatuation, mania. Fate, foolishness.

The Magician I

"The painter has the Universe in his mind and hands."

—Leonardo di ser Piero da Vinci (1452–1519)

According to the *Dossier Secrets*, a collection of documents deposited in the French national library in the 1960s, Leonardo da Vinci was the twelfth Grand Master of the Priory of Sion, presiding over the order from 1510–1519. There are, in actuality, a total of three separate lists of Grand Masters spanning years from 1188 to 1989; however, the *Dossier Secrets* collection is said to have been deposited in the Bibliotèque Nationale de Paris by none other than the Priory itself and contained within the material is a list of Grand Masters reaching as far back to the Crusades. The list of twenty-six Grand Masters includes prominent historical members of the arts, well-known alchemists, and purported "blood-line" nobility and royalty. This illustrious list certainly goes so far as to demonstrate the ideals of the Priory of Sion and Leonardo da Vinci, amongst the other luminaries of art, music, science, and literature, is generally recognized as one of the greatest minds since the dawn of recorded history. His allegorical and esoteric religious works defied ecclesiastical doctrine under the very nose of an unsuspecting Mother Church whose clergy often commissioned those very same masterpieces such as the *Virgin of the Rocks* (1483), *The Last Supper* (1495), and *John the Baptist* (1513). Leonardo's proclivities certainly correspond with the theological and philosophical tenets of the Priory.

Leonardo has been associated with the mysterious Shroud of Turin. The revered relic portrays an eerie image that many believe depicts the corpse of a crucified Christ inexplicably emblazoned upon the ancient funerary cloth wrap. There are those who proclaim the infamous image to be a hoax; that the image may be a Leonardo invention. According to this theory, the Renaissance master truly was one of few in the world possessing the technical and creative ability to engineer such a brilliant, provocative project for which the artist himself may have been the model. Some say it was Leonardo's intention to portray the image of Templar Grand Master Jacques de Molay. To the contrary, there exists an ideology that declares the most accomplished skills and talents of the Renaissance could never have produced such a colossal technological feat as at that time it would have been impossible, even for a genius such as Leonardo da Vinci.

Meaning

Archangel: Raphael
Cabala: Path 11, Kether–Chockmah
Element: Air
Hebrew: Aleph

In the continental tradition, the first Major Arcanum is *Le Jongleur* (juggler) or *Le Bateleur* (trickster), essentially a classic troubadour. These travelling medieval entertainers and poets were also keepers of esoteric knowledge that they shared with the initiated as they journeyed from town to court. This first trump is known typically as The Magician in English-speaking countries as he evolved into an adept under the influence of Victorian occultists.

His table laden with devices, which vary in different deck types, however, point to the early Italian decks as generating the theme of utilizing suit symbols as the magician's implements, which is a consistent thread within the tapestry of the Major Arcana. The earliest extant versions (Visconti-Sforza) present a seated Magician. Present on his table are the tools of his trade: a cup, coins, and knife—his hand grasps a thin, vertical wand. Cups, Pentacles, Swords, and Wands. These are integral during Masonic and Golden Dawn rituals and can be interpreted suggesting chivalry tied to the Knights Templar: Cups—the holy grail, Coins—Templar wealth, Wands—the flowering tree of the bloodline, and Swords—knightly weaponry. These suit symbols are also alchemical in nature as their related elements form the crux of alchemy: Cups/Water/Iron, Pentacles/Earth/Copper, Wands/Fire/Gold, and Swords/Air/Lead.

A magician masters cause and effect, commanding thought into action producing desired results. The element Air articulates this talent: the magician creates something out of nothing. It is a God-like talent, the incorporeal quality of miracles. Metaphysical magicians do more than conjure, they enact their will either through themselves or a higher power (theurgy). The Hebrew correspondence Aleph is first of the three mother letters: aleph, mem, and shin. Aleph represents an ox (strength and perseverance) and its derivative aluph means master or lord. The eleventh path from Kether to Chokmah represents the transition from 1 (the spark of creation) into 2 (masculine formation). As a magician expresses thought willed into action, so this path takes the abstract of Kether and translates it into the tangible. Archangel Raphael lords over the ruling planet Mercury, the god of magick and messages.

Keywords

As above, so below! Microcosm of the macrocosm. Invention, new beginnings, self-control. Action, manifestation. Willpower, ego. New lodgings or home, change of residence.

The High Priestess II

"She had discovered that her love of knowing was not unnatural or sinful but the direct consequence of a God-given ability to reason."

—Donna Woolfolk Cross, *Pope Joan*

The persistent legend of a female pope first appears in Dominican Jean de Mailly's record of Metz, *Chronica Universalis Mettensis*, written in the early thirteenth century. In his recount, the female pope is not named, and the events are set in 1099. This is an interesting coincidence as this date coincides with the victorious campaign led by Godfrey de Bouillon in Jerusalem, the founding of the Templar Knights, and the building of the Abbey Notre Dame du Mont de Sion (Our Lady of Mount Sion). The abbey was constructed on the site of the ruined Byzantine basilica known as the Mother of all Churches, which lay in crumbles, perched atop Mount Sion south of Jerusalem. According to Jean de Mailly: "Concerning a certain Pope or rather female Pope, who is not set down in the list of popes or Bishops of Rome, because she was a woman who disguised herself as a man and became, by her character and talents, a curial secretary, then a Cardinal and finally Pope. One day, while mounting a horse, she gave birth to a child. Immediately, by Roman justice, she was bound by the feet to a horse's tail and dragged and stoned by the people for half a league, and, where she died, there she was buried, and at the place is written: Oh Peter, Father of Fathers, Betray the childbearing of the woman Pope." During that period, the four-day fast called the "fast of the female Pope" was first recognized.

Many agree the continental Tarots dating as far back as the earliest examples contain an image of the infamous Pope Joan—La Papessa, known in most modern Tarots as The High Priestess. In most of the continental varieties, especially the Visconti, the female pope definitely appears pregnant and in other images she could be construed as such. Other artistic examples abound, clues lay hidden in ancient parchment much to the chagrin of the church and its papacy, which dismisses Pope Joan entirely. Statues of the female pope had been defaced, manipulated, or destroyed but several still exist. None other than Gian Lorenzo Bernini (1598–1680), brilliant sculptor to the Vatican, fashioned a statue of a woman regaled in proper papal attire that can be viewed at St. Peter's Basilica in Rome today. The church explains away the statue as representing the Mother church or a depiction of a previous pope's niece.

Meaning

Archangel: Gabriel
Astrology: The Moon
Cabala: Path 12, Kether–Binah
Element: Water
Hebrew: Beth

The first Tarots complete with inscriptions are believed to be the early Marseille woodcuts. The female figure popularly referred to as The High Priestess was originally bedecked in papal attire and titled *La Papesse*, the Popess. This may propose female equality practiced among the Cathars of northern Italy and southern France. Some say The High Priestess refers to the legend of Pope Joan, a historically debated figure who, disguised as a man, rose to rule Christianity, the only woman ever to do so. More intriguing yet, Manfreda Visconti da Pirovano was to be declared Pope in Milan on Easter 1300 during a new age of heretical theology. The church responded that year by immolating Manfreda and others of her sect, the Guglielmites. Could Manfreda be the woman portrayed on the Tarot Popess card? Manfreda was first cousin to anti-papist ruler Matteo Visconti; the Visconti family is well known for its commission of Tarot decks that bear the family name.

La Papesse is a thoroughly and wondrously sacrilegious card. Trump number II stands out in early Major Arcana that was festooned with Christian accoutrements. When these decks first circulated, the church was waging a holy war against the Christian Gnostic sects and these images that depicted women as the most high of the Catholic priestly caste were heresy of the highest degree. Northern Italy was notoriously anti-papist as was the south of France, the areas where Catharism flourished and was then tragically obliterated into the pages of history.

The High Priestess is governed by the feminine forces of the Moon and ruled by Archangel Gabriel, patron of magick and mysticism, the home, and women's affairs. The second trump teaches the initiate the meaning of The Magician's credo: "That which is born in the heights is echoed in the depths"—"As above, so below." The twelfth path is the way of Understanding, glowing consciousness, and remembrance. The Hebrew letter Beth refers to a household structure or lower dwelling for God's house of prayer for all people. The dwelling can also refer to the actual Tabernacle or Temple, which the High Priestess safeguards as she gazes serenely, knowingly, embracing the knowledge of all ages while enthroned at its entrance for all eternity.

Keywords

Inner wisdom, deep knowledge, keen intuition, hidden meaning. Divine enlightenment, instinctive understanding. Innate sensitivity, guardianship, serenity. Revelation, sanctuary.

The Empress III

"What your fair hand has gathered as your choice, the white rose. There slumbers a pale dreamy red that seems like to the dreamy beauty of this garden. Give me one other yet! Also a white one, so will I then with both my bonnet deck, and think I wear your colors."

—From the play *King René's Daughter* (1845) by Henrik Hertz

Yolande d'Anjou, born of the House of Valois-Anjou, was also known as de Lorraine and de Bar. She was born in Nancy, France, in 1428 where she lived until her death in 1483. She was the daughter of Isabella, Duchess of Lorraine, and René d'Anjou (King of Naples, Duke of Anjou, Bar and Lorraine, Count of Provence). Her younger sister Margaret was Queen consort of Henry VI of England. Yolande wed her cousin Frederick II, Count of Vaudémont in 1445. The marriage was a dynastic alliance arranged to end the disagreements between King René and Frederick's father, Antoine of Vaudémont, regarding the succession to the Duchy of Lorraine.

The marriage was prolific, producing six children: René II, Nicholas—Lord of Joinville and Bauffremont, Peter, Joan, Yolande, and Margaret. This progeny produced historically significant issue such as Mary, Queen of Scots, who was descended from René II.

According to the *Dossier Secrets*, Yolande d'Anjou was the tenth Grand Master of the Priory of Sion, succeeding her father, King René. Upon her father's death in 1480, she began her rule over the order until her own demise in 1483. She was preceded in Priory office by two of her ancestors over one hundred-fifty years prior to her ascendancy, Edouard de Bar (Grandmaster 1307–36) and Jeanne de Bar (Grandmaster 1336–51). A common thread can be seen weaving throughout the early Grandmasters of the Priory, especially the first six. Although it was deposed in the eighth century, the Merovingian bloodline did not become extinct. Generational dynastic alliances and intermarriages continued the bloodline in noble and royal families, among which is included the Houses of Lorraine, Valois, and Anjou. These noble and royal houses include designations such as de Bar, de Gisors, and de Saint-Clair (Sinclair).

Of the first ten Grand Masters of the Priory of Sion, it appears four were women—women elected to high office. During this period (1188–1483), women were severely oppressed by the Catholic Church. The election of these women clearly demonstrates the forward thinking and enlightened philosophy embraced by the Priory, which is said to have been practiced by Jesus himself as demonstrated by his true teachings.

Meaning

Archangel: Anael
Astrology: Mars
Cabala: Path 13, Kether–Tiphareth
Element: Fire
Hebrew: Gimel

She is Mother of Earth clothed with the Sun. Her title, The Empress, is a signature that has withstood the test of Tarot time, rarely varying. In many decks, the red-headed Empress is attired in regal raiment and occupies her place on the throne of nature; she almost always appears heavily pregnant.

Early Italian decks present an expectant Empress accompanied by a young female child. In the Cary-Yale Visconti deck she is accompanied by four servants. However, this is not seen in other early decks of this genre. The card's ruling red planet Mars embodies an aggressive nature, however, it also symbolizes tenacity and courage—two qualities a protective mother demonstrates. The Empress is often portrayed with a shield appearing on the left side of the card, leaning against her throne. Interestingly, the left pillar of the Tree of Life is the feminine aspect. The traditional continental Tarots portray the shield as bearing an eagle, both a heraldic device and a Masonic symbol.

The Hebrew letter associated with Mars is Gimel. The Sephir Yetzirah states: "He produced Gimel, and referred it to Health; He crowned it, combined and joined with it Mars in the Universe…" The impact of Mars as the bright red blood or life-force of our cosmos creates a planet that is a macrocosm of life within the water-filled womb. The literal meaning of Gimel is *camel*, a desert animal known for its ability to store great amounts of water. In many desert countries the camel is looked upon as the Carrier of Life.

Anael, the archangel of Love, is associated with the Greek/Roman gods Aphrodite, Venus, and Cupid. The thirteenth path of Imagination and Unification lies upwards on the central pillar of the Tree of Life and connects god-head Kether to the brilliant beauty of Tipharet. Three is the number of manifestation; "one" joins with "two" and gives birth to "three." The Empress embodies this fertile expression. The number three belongs to the concord of 3-6-9. It is no coincidence these numbers resemble each other. The upper portion of 3 could be rotated to the left and downward, forming a 6, which when turned upside down creates a 9. Their meanings also complement each other: 3= creativity, 6 = birth, 9 = completion.

Keywords

The embodied feminine principle and motherhood. Fertility, wealth, fruition, abundance. Procreation, beauty, maternity. Domestic harmony, understanding, nurturing. Sensual, natural.

The Emperor IIII

"He who drinks well will see God. He who quaffs at a single draught will see God and the Magdalene"

—the inscription on a chalice belonging to "Good King René"

René d'Anjou (1408–1480), ninth Grand Master of the Priory of Sion (1418–80) was a French royal possessed of many titles including titular King of Jerusalem. He was likewise considered a man ahead of his time, less a warrior than a consummate artist and intellectual. An educated and literate man, the king was a prolific writer, an erudite poet, and avid painter. King René anticipated the profound effects of the courtly Renaissance movement of northern Italy, and as such sought to promote a progressive society with an advancement toward understanding and awareness. The Good King was immersed in esoteric teachings and mystical traditions; his court included physician Jean Saint-Rémy, a well-known Cabalist and Jewish astrologer who happened to be the grandfather of Nostradamus, the famous sixteenth century prophet and forecaster.

René practiced a scholarly approach to Arthurian folklore and grail romances with a preoccupation towards the latter. It is said he was in possession of a magnificent cup made of red porphyry that he obtained during a visit to Marseilles where, according to tradition, Mary Magdalene came ashore bearing the grail. René maintained it was the very cup used at the wedding at Cana. The mysterious inscription on the cup read "He who drinks well will see God. He who quaffs at a single draught will see God and the Magdalene."

King René could definitely be regarded as significant motivation behind the Renaissance movement as his many Italian possessions would attest to. He spent some years in Italy at the estates of the ruling Sforza family and through them René established a relationship with the patrons of the Renaissance, the Medicis of Florence. There is good reason to determine it was René's inspiration which impelled the Medicis to embark on ambitious and groundbreaking projects that were fated to transform Western civilization. During René's tenure in Italy, Cosimo Medici began collecting. After five years of diligent assembling, the Italian nobleman founded Europe's first public archive, the Library of San Marco, defying the church's long held monopoly on education.

Meaning

Archangel: Michael
Astrology: Sun
Cabala: Path 14, Chokmah–Binah
Element: Fire
Hebrew: Daleth

Usually depicted in esoteric decks as seated upon a square stone or throne, The Emperor is customarily depicted as a scepter-wielding, mature, bearded monarch. In many cards, a shield emblazoned with a heraldic eagle leans against his regal seat. This illustrates the king has accrued years of wisdom and experience. The square is a symbolic Masonic staple (the square and compass) and a numerological implement consistent with the number four, the number of strength, substance, practicality, and stability—four attributes of a moral sovereign. The Emperor occupies the fourteenth path on the Cabalistic Tree, the path of Illumined

Consciousness reflected in the number four. There are four qualities of the enlightened soul. Eliphas Levi taught true wisdom cannot be attained without these attributes, namely the power to Know, the power to Dare, the power to Act, and the power to Keep Silent. According to the Book of Enoch, "Without these four powers the Soul cannot reach mastery." The Hebrew *Daleth* means "The Door"—this path opens the door to wise leadership and logical decision making. The Emperor has the necessary knowledge and temerity to cross the threshold of Daleth, entering this path of wisdom and rational thinking. His focused character serves him well and reflects his governance; he is a wellspring from which sage advice may be drawn. The ruling archangel Michael is associated with the Sun and is the angel of righteousness, mercy, and repentance. The Sun lends its superlative industrious energy to this Major Arcanum and expresses itself as sheer willpower and creativity, literally feeding latent kernels of existence into fully flowering explosions of life on so many evolutionary levels.

Keywords | Worldly wisdom. Law, order, structure. Stability, fortification, protection. Reason, intellect, principle. Paternity, masculinity, virility, power. Leadership, dominion, command.

The Hierophant V

"One must be firm and unchanging with regard to the end but gentle and humble as to the means."

—St. Vincent de Paul (1581–1660)

St. Vincent de Paul appears on an additional list of purported Sion Grand Masters. There are a total of three rosters: the *Dossiers Secrets,* which resides in the Bibliotèque Nationale, and two lists that are retained by the Priory itself. It is one of these Priory registers where we find St. Vincent de Paul. According to this document he could have been the seventeenth or eighteenth Grand Master. This list contradicts the *Dossiers Secrets* in that Paul would have led the organization at the same time as either Johann Valentin Andrea or Robert Boyle as they are recorded on the *Dossiers Secrets.*

Priory documents maintain the fraternity cloaked its identity for political intentions during the mid-seventeenth century, creating for itself a façade. These papers refer repeatedly to a secret society known as the Compagnie du Saint-Sacrament, an historic organization founded between 1627 and 1630 by like-minded noblemen and clerics. The fraternity operated under the guise of charity and assistance. Two of its notable members were the progressive priests Father Jean-Jaques Olier and St. Vincent de Paul. The latter was a Catholic priest renowned for his charitable works for which he was canonized in 1737. It is known of St. Vincent de Paul that he worked towards the equality of the genders within the church, elevating the role of women. He was a co-founder of the Daughters of Charity, an organization that provided relief to the destitute but was also an attempt to promote the prominence of women within the Catholic establishment.

As a young priest, Paul was abducted off the shores of Marseilles and held in slavery by different captors. Some say that is the official version; he was actually on a secret mission devoted to an esoteric education. There are those who believe Paul had not been abducted, but instead spent his time in Notre Dame de Marceille (Limoux), not in Marseille as the official story states. In the Castle of Barbarie, Vincent de Paul studied alchemy under the tutelage of Jean the Alchemist, very "un-saintly" arts indeed. The Castle had been known as the "Occult Bastion of France" and was ordered dismantled by Prime Minister Cardinal Jules Mazarin, the very cleric whose deposition was the sole objective of the Compagnie du Saint-Sacrament!

Meaning

Archangel: Samael
Astrology: Aries
Cabala: Path 15, Chokmah–Tiphareth
Element: Fire
Hebrew: Heh

This card in many decks represents the pope as leader of the Church of Peter, the Church of Rome. In many traditional portrayals a key or two keys are present; these are thought to represent the keys to heaven or the Mother Church. The fifth trump has varied through the years, reflecting the surrounding political and religious environment and bearing different papal devices, accoutrements, and apparel in different decks through the centuries.

Customarily, the card depicts a papal rector attended by lower ranking clerics, tonsured novices, or pages, however, in earlier decks the pope appears by himself.

In Freemasonry, five is a sacred number especially significant in the Fellow Craft's Degree where five are required to hold a Lodge, and the five winding stairs are referred to as the orders of architecture and the human senses. Five, the number of humanity and man, is a profoundly occult digit, inexorably linked to the pentagram and beautifully demonstrated by Leonardo da Vinci's *Vitruvian Man*. The trump became known as The Hierophant (Greek origin) when the hermetic community of Britain adopted the Tarot as their own during the dawn of the twentieth century. Archangel Samael rules this trump; he is an angel who warns against the corrupting forces of power and wealth, often the downfall of those previously installed within the papacy. The card is ruled by Aries, the first sign of the zodiac, and seasonally associated with spring. The Hierophant is the high priest who presides over the celebration of the equinox. Aries is governed by Mars, the planet of activity and assertiveness. The Hierophant travels path 15, the path of intuition, on the Cabalistic Tree. His Hebraic correspondence is Heh, which literally means window and represents divine breath, revelation, and light… returning to God by means of the transmitting power of Spirit. Intuition is a two way window used to peer into the soul.

Keywords	Inspiration, morality, understanding. Teach deeper truths. Aware of one's station. Mercy and forgiveness. Service to community. Journey for veracity and wisdom. Traditional, ritualistic.

The Lovers VI

"To convince devout Catholic priests that Jesus was married, the evidence would have to be overwhelming. At least the body of Mary Magdalene, along with stone tablets and relics associated with her wedding to Jesus would build toward an undeniable physical proof that this interpretation of Christianity was the correct one."

—Robert Howells, *Inside the Priory of Sion*, (Watkins Publishing 2011)

Could recently discovered ancient gospels and documents, known today as the Nag Hammadi Library and the Dead Sea Scrolls, be scripture intentionally omitted from original biblical texts? These manuscripts offer a different view of Jesus' life lived as a man fully human. By denying Jesus the complete dimension of his humanity, society of old as well as today suffers oppression, bigotry, and violence. Can anyone apply a volume to the amount of blood shed in the name of flawed theology? It is tragically impossible.

In Jesus' day, the designation "rabbi" was not a moniker bestowed on unmarried men of the clergy. Robert Howells in *Inside the Priory of Sion* says, "According to Jewish law at the time 'rabbi' was a title that could only be conferred upon married men." Several entries in the New Testament refer to Jesus as "rabbi." Of great significance is the meeting in the garden where Mary Magdalene is the first to see Jesus after the Crucifixion; upon recognizing him she rushed to him as she cried "Rabboni!"

There is indication the wedding at Cana (John 2:1–11) was Jesus' own wedding. Jesus was specifically "called" to this celebration; there is debate regarding this invitation; however, a request in an official capacity would have been out of character as he had not yet begun his ministry. More curious is his mother's presence, ordering servants so her son may expedite the wine situation. These are not the actions of attending guests as two visitors would not take on the responsibility of catering the wedding. That service is the obligation of the wedding hosts and the servants dutifully comply with Mary and Jesus' orders. The wedding at Cana could very well have been Jesus' own nuptials, and if so it would have been his responsibility to restock the wine. Should Jesus have indeed been married, then there would have been issue. If Jesus were truly King of the Jews, as it is claimed he was, these children would have been of royal lineage capable of producing the same. It is presumed by many, in resources too numerous to list here, that one of the Priory's many tasks through the years was and is that of protecting Jesus' sacred bloodline.

Meaning

Archangel: Anael
Astrology: Taurus
Cabala: Path 16, Chokmah–Chesed
Element: Earth
Hebrew: Vav

The Chymical Wedding of Christian Rosenkreutz was edited in 1616 Strasbourg, Germany, although the story takes place over 150 years earlier. The manuscript is attributed to Christian Rosenkreutz, the founder of the Rosicrucian Order; however, the actual writer is most likely Johann Valentin Andreae, seventeenth

Priory Grand Master according to the *Dossiers Secrets*. The story, spanning seven days divided into seven chapters, narrates the tale of Rosenkreutz' journey to court to assist the alchemical wedding of the king and queen. The story begins near Easter and in the final chapter Rosenkreutz is knighted in 1459. It was on Easter 1459 the Constitution of Freemasons in Strasburg was first signed.

Chymical Wedding is a source of inspiration for alchemists as it represents the ultimate alchemical achievement, the "Sacred Marriage" or "hieros gamos." Alchemically speaking, the hieros gamos is a union between humanity and divinity, bringing together the polar opposites of male and female. This energy creates a dynamic more potent than the individual alone.

This philosophy is reflected in The Lovers trump. The Marseille versions added a significant second woman to their "L'Amoureux" card. The card pictures a young man positioned between two women, the woman on the left being an older woman sporting a crown or wreath, and the woman on the right being a younger woman, arm entwined with the young man's own and appearing to hide a pregnancy. Tarotists interpret this to indicate choices. This may be as the Cabalistic sixteenth path occupied by The Lovers is that of conscience, choices, and consequences. However, the card takes on new meaning considering the French Magdalene tradition, which originated in Marseilles. "L'Amoureux" may actually depict the Sacred Lovers receiving the blessing of the young man's mother as they embark on their lives betrothed as one, having chosen each other. Taurus lends its attributes of romance and courtship; its ruling planet Venus (ruled by the archangel Anael) adds its dimension of feminine passion and desire. The card's numeric station of "six" is the number of love, marriage, and procreation. The Hebrew letter Vav means "tent peg" or "nail," implements that keep the lovers' house from collapse.

Keywords

Mystical union, the bonding of opposites both externally and internally. Marriage, soul mates, attraction. Desire, affection. Faith, trust, harmony, balance. Innocence. Correct paths.

The Chariot VII

"Gravity explains the motions of the planets, but it cannot explain who sets the planets in motion."

—Isaac Newton (1642–1727)

Sir Isaac Newton, the historically noted English scientist and mathematician, established many theories and universal laws with which today's academics are well versed. However, not as well-known are Sir Isaac's works that would now be classified as occult studies. These hermetic explorations examined chronology, alchemy, and biblical interpretation (especially the Apocalypse, considered Gnostic text). Newton's scientific effort may have been of lesser personal significance to him, as he was driven to rediscover esoteric wisdom of the ancients. In this sense, some believe that any reference to a "Newtonian Worldview" as being purely mechanical in nature is somewhat inaccurate. John Maynard Keynes (1883–1946), a British economist whose ideas have fundamentally affected the theory and practice of modern macroeconomics, purchased and studied

Newton's alchemical works in 1942. The economist preached: "Newton was not the first of the age of reason, he was the last of the magicians."

Newton is listed as the nineteenth Grand Master of the Priory of Sion in the *Dossier Secrets*, leading the secret society during the years 1691–1727. He is known for his theories regarding gravity, light, and the laws governing motion and thermodynamics. He claimed descent from ancient Scottish nobility and, as an aristocratic Englishman, he attended Cambridge University. He was inducted into the Royal Society in 1672 at age thirty, where he met his contemporary, fellow alchemist, and preceding Grand Master of Sion, Robert Boyle, in 1673. Newton also belonged to a quasi-Masonic organization called the Gentleman's Club of Spalding. Newton was clearly interested in subjects to which Freemasonry addresses itself and authored *The Chronology of Ancient Kingdoms Amended*, which traces the origins of the institution of monarchy, especially the Jewish monarchy of King David. Authors Baigent, Lincoln, and Leigh describe Newton as attempting to establish the preeminence of Israel over other cultures of antiquity. Like many Freemasons, Newton believed that the ancient Jewish mysteries contained true revelations and divine secrets, but that they had largely been corrupted over time by the editors of the Torah and the Holy Bible, views reflected in the philosophy of the Priory of Sion.

Meaning

Archangel: Raphael
Astrology: Gemini
Cabala: Path 17, Binah–Tiphareth
Element: Air
Hebrew: Zayin

Plato, in his dialogue *Phaedrus*, uses his Chariot allegory to explain his view of the human soul. Plato paints the picture of a charioteer driving a chariot pulled by two winged horses: "First the charioteer of the human soul drives a pair, and secondly one of the horses is noble and of noble breed, but the other quite the opposite in breed and character. Therefore in our case the driving is necessarily difficult and troublesome." The charioteer represents intellect and reason, qualities that guide the soul to truth; one horse represents rational or moral impulse while the other represents the soul's irrational passions and cravings. The charioteer drives the chariot/soul, keeping the horses reined in, proceeding towards spiritual enlightenment.

The seventh trump, The Chariot, appears to be a direct reflection of this Platonic philosophy. It is another Arcanum that has experienced changes over the centuries, though it seems for more esoteric reasons rather than political motives. This card's appearance heralds a hero's triumphal return; the trump embraces a victorious mood. Another analogy looks at the comparison between the Chariot and the church: in the *Visconti-Sforza Tarot*, the white horses that guide the Chariot have wings (Plato). This would put forward something more esoteric than chronological. A chariot was often used to symbolize the church acting as a vehicle to convey the faithful to heaven. The image is suggested in the prophecy of Ezekiel and the Chariot of Fire, which carried Elijah off to heaven. Author Margaret Starbird believes The Chariot to be a representation of the Knights Templar returning from the Crusades, bearing treasure and secrets plundered from the rubble beneath the Temple of Solomon.

The card's zodiacal attribute of Gemini and its archangelic correspondence Raphael are both ruled by the planet of movement and magick, the Messenger of the Gods, Mercury. Gemini lends its characteristics of communication, wisdom, and intellect to The Chariot for without these qualities there can be no victory. The Chariot rides the seventeenth Cabalistic path of Consciousness of the Senses, the ability to experience accomplishment and triumph. The Hebraic attribute of this card, Zayin, means sword, the instrument aiding in the attainment of victory.

Keywords

Movement, forward momentum, activity. Triumph over difficulties or moral complications. Progress, travel, journeys. Mastery and control. Focus on goals.

Justice VIII

> "It is probable that 'Scottish Rite' Freemasonry was originally promulgated, if not indeed devised, by Charles Radclyffe."
>
> —Baigent, Lincoln, and Leigh, *Holy Blood, Holy Grail*, 1982

Charles Radclyffe (1693–1746), is listed in the *Dossiers Secrets* as the twentieth Grand Master of the Priory of Sion (1727–46). His birth was royal, if slightly ignoble, as his mother was the illegitimate child of King Charles II Stuart of Britain—the next-to-last Stuart (Stewart) monarch to reign over England, Ireland, and Scotland. As a cousin of Bonnie Prince Charlie (Prince Charles Edward Stuart, a son of the exiled sovereign Stuarts), Radclyffe was understandably sympathetic to the Stuart cause and spent much of his life in an effort to reinstate the Stuarts upon the thrones of Britain. In 1715, Radclyffe was captured during the Scottish rebellion, imprisoned, and handed a death sentence alongside his brother, James. James Radclyffe was executed. Charles, however, made a daring escape from Newgate prison with the help of the Earl of Lichfield, after which he joined the ranks of Jacobites and soon became secretary to the "Young Pretender" to the British sovereignty, Bonnie Prince Charlie.

The Jacobites were adherents of a political movement that sought to restore the Roman Catholic Stuarts to the thrones of England, Scotland, and Ireland. The movement took its name from "Jacobus," the Latinized form of James, and refers to a series of uprisings between 1688 and 1746. In 1660, after the death of English "dictator" Oliver Cromwell, the Royalists claimed control and King Charles II was restored to the throne of England. His brother became King James VII of Scotland and II of England when Charles II died in 1685. At this time, English Protestants besought James's nephew and son-in-law, Prince William of Orange, to come protect the Anglican Church. King James fled to France with his family and Dutch Prince William and his wife Mary II were offered the throne. Many believed James to be the rightful king, taking upon themselves the title of "Jacobites." Scots loyal to King James, his son, and his grandson Bonnie Prince Charlie would battle for the exiled Stuarts in a series of Jacobite Risings.

The final uprising, the Battle of Culloden Moor of 1746, saw the "Young Pretender" disastrously defeated and Charles Radclyffe met the headsman's axe a few months later at the Tower of London. Of interest: the House of Stuart is purported to be of direct Merovingian descent.

Meaning

Archangel: Gabriel
Astrology: Cancer
Cabala: Path 18, Binah–Geburah
Element: Water
Hebrew: Heth

Modern Tarot presents three out of four cardinal virtues within the Major Arcana. These Christian merits were originally derived from Plato's identification of the four cardinal virtues describing a virtuous and just city-state in his dialogue *The Republic*—"Clearly, then, it will be wise, brave, temperate, and just." The term "cardinal" comes from the Latin cardo (hinge); the cardinal virtues represent the four hinges upon which the door of moral life swings. The four cardinal virtues are: Justice, Strength, Prudence, and Temperance. Iconic symbols of these virtues appear in this exact sequence on the tomb of Pope Clement II (1005–1046), one of several progressive popes from Germany whom it is suspected was assassinated. Is it coincidence the virtues appearing in the traditional Major Arcana also appear in this order (minus Prudence) as Justice VIII, Strength XI, and Temperance XIIII? What became of Prudence? She does appear in one deck, The Minchiate Tarot of the Renaissance, separated by eight cards from the other Cardinal Virtues, which appear in reverse sequence: Temperance VI, Strength VII, and Justice of VIII. There is no pat response to the question of the missing virtue, but there are theories. Occultist Gareth Knight, using the enigmatic Gringonneur/Charles VI deck, suggests The World card indicates Prudence as only four Major Arcana have stylized aureoles: Justice, Strength, Temperance, and the World. Another theory proposes Prudence is represented by The Hermit; however, this contradicts the traditional representation of the Virtues as female.

Archangel Gabriel gives Justice the gifts of hope, truth, and righteousness. Gabriel is the alchemist of karmic reciprocity. The Hebrew *Heth* (fence) denotes intuition and understanding, qualities inherent in true justice. Intuition is the wisdom of the soul. It discriminates unerringly between veracity and falsehood. Path eighteen on the Tree of Life is one of strength and weakness divided by the fence of Heth. Justice's scales maintain the balance. Cancer establishes Justice as tempered by mercy, for without this quality, Justice may be blindfolded. Because of the ruling influence of Cancer, Justice is infused with intuitive insight and the ability to delegate with fairness regardless of subjective agenda.

Keywords

Eradication of bias, prejudice, and misconceptions. Good is victorious over evil. Harmony, honesty, integrity, honor. Fairness, objectivity, trials. Logic, reason, reconciliation.

The Hermit VIIII

"It is time! It is time to liberate the Holy City where Christ was crucified and resurrected from the hands of the Saracens. It is time to restore the Holy Temple in Jerusalem!"

—Peter the Hermit

Peter the Hermit (1050–1115), was a priest and Calabrian monk from Amiens who was said to be tutor to Liberator of Jerusalem, Godfrey de Bouillon-Lorraine. He was a key figure during the First Crusade and many academics view the evangelizing cleric as truly initiating the First Crusade. The accounts of William of Tyre indicate descendants of first crusaders believed Peter to be its designer. It has been suggested Peter the Hermit's fame found its spark in the legions of commoners summoned to take up arms by the monk's fiery sermons preached throughout the country-side, bidding them to fight alongside the crusading knights against the Seljuk Empire and Saracen armies. The idolization of Peter the Hermit had begun and paralleled the glorification of Godfrey de Bouillon-Lorraine. The First Crusade (1098–99) was wrought with horrendous violence, as were most sieges of the day. But, the objective was achieved and Jerusalem was liberated from Muslim control and lay in the hands of Christian nobility. To this day, the title "King of Jerusalem" is bestowed upon descendants of the royal House of Lorraine.

However, it appears Peter the Hermit had an agenda, an agenda that may have seeded the formation of the Priory of Sion in emancipated Jerusalem. This plan was to place a scion of the Merovingian bloodline upon the throne of David in Jerusalem. In doing so, Peter, his political allies, and noble patrons anticipated the reestablishment of royal Davidic heritage in Jerusalem. This event would help bring about the faith of the supporting gentry, the true Christianity that had gone underground with its original teachings supplanted by the corrupted traditions that had become the Church of Rome. It was Peter's belief the time had come to restore the royal bloodline of King David to the throne of Jerusalem. One thousand years had passed since Romans had sacked the holy city and sacred temple. Christians and Jews alike fled, scattering themselves in pockets throughout the world in Diaspora, taking with them the old ways, the original mystical philosophies and theosophical wisdom. In this manner, the true meaning of Christianity was kept alive under the very nose of a church that would twist those teachings into tools of oppression, misogyny, and discrimination.

Meaning

Archangel: Michael
Astrology: Leo
Cabala: Path 19, Geburah-Chesed
Element: Fire
Hebrew: Teth

The Olympian Greek god Hermes, son of Zeus and Maia, was a divine messenger and god of the ancient sciences and commerce. Quick and cunning, Hermes was able to move swiftly between the worlds of humans and gods, delivering messages from the deities. He was the direct link between mortals and the Olympians. From this god derives the word "hermetic," meaning completely sealed (or alone, hidden, or secret) and denotes the occult sciences or alchemy. Hermes is identified by Neoplatonists, mystics, and alchemists with the Egyptian god Thoth as Hermes Trismegistus: Thrice-Great Hermes the Magician.

From this, a relationship with the ninth trump—The Hermit—can be observed although "hermit" has a different Latin etymology. A hermit is a spiritual or mystic recluse… he or she is "sealed off" from the outside world. The Hermit epitomizes the ultimate oath of the initiate: silence.

The astrological correspondence of Leo has several connotations. The fire of Leo burns in The Hermit's lantern. Some decks replace the flame with the Magen David (RWS). The Magen David is often associated with the Lion of Judah—Jesus the Christ—whom many academics surmise was not born a Pisces but a Leo. Interestingly, there is also the story of a famous twelfth-century hermit who preached a philosophy counter to church dogma. The hermit's name was Waldensius of Lyon and he founded the Waldensian movement, declared heretical by the church. Its followers were known as "The Leonese." The word Lyon is directly related to the word lion, which is symbolic of the zodiac Leo. This sign is ruled by the Archangel Michael and his fiery sword; Leo lends a blaze of dynamism and magick. The number nine embodies the power of mystery, secrets, and silence, the ninth hour being one dedicated to meditation, rest, and reflection. The Hebrew letter Teth reveals the distinction between good and evil, light and darkness, and the temptations and weaknesses that can plague the soul. The nineteenth path on the Tree of Life is the creative journey of spiritual fulfillment and embodies the secrets of all spiritual activity. This Path of Introspection is the road where belief systems lead spiritual exploration deep into the subconscious mind, probing existence and searching for life's answers.

Keywords

Solitude, isolation, reflection, meditation, contemplation. Restraint, control, discretion. Solace, moderation, prudence. Spiritual or mystical quest. Suspicion, caution, examination.

The Wheel of Fortune X

> "…some of Nostradamus' prophecies were not prophecies but referred, quite explicitly, to the past—to the Knights Templar, the Merovingian dynasty, the history of the House of Lorraine."
>
> —Baigent, Lincoln, and Leigh, *Holy Blood, Holy Grail*, 1982

Michel de Nostredame (1503–1566), known by the Latinized "Nostradamus," was the French seer celebrated for published prophecies that have since become legendary. Born in upper-class Provence, young Michel was highly educated having entered the University of Avignon to study for his baccalaureate, after which he traveled the countryside researching herbal remedies to aid in curing bubonic plague. In 1529, he entered the University of Montpellier to further his education with a doctorate in medicine. Nostradamus was expelled after his university admission when it was discovered he was an apothecary, a practice banned by the university. After his expulsion, Nostradamus continued his homeopathy and became famous for concocting "rose pills," immunity against the plague. However, despite his education and studies, Nostradamus is inexorably associated with the mystery of his intricate prophecies.

    Less known is Nostradamus may well have been an agent for the Priory of Sion. During his lifetime a ferocious struggle ensued augmented by the royal Houses of Lorraine and Guise to exterminate the Valois dynasty and return Lorraine to the French throne. It is rumored the Priory assisted in this power bid as members of the House of Lorraine had been previous PoS Grand Masters. Nostradamus was astrologer to the French court and advisor to the Queen consort Catharine de Medici. In his capacity as court astrologer, Nostradamus would have been in an ideal position to manipulate events sympathetic to the cause of the House of Lorraine and supply sensitive information. Nostradamus' famous quatrains may not have been prophecies at all, but encoded messages intended to aid his benefactors' machinations. During previous years, the seer spent considerable time in Lorraine as an initiate where it is said he learned ominous secrets, which included an ancient arcane book upon which he based his future works. This book divulged to him a mysterious place—the Abbey of Orval, a donation from the family of Godfrey de Bouillon and suggested to be the birthplace of the Priory of Sion. The Abbey became Nostradamus' sanctuary and scriptorium and was said to have housed Templar treasure. The seer continues to be known to this day as the Prophet of Orval—the Valley of Gold.

Meaning

Archangel: Raphael
Astrology: Virgo
Cabala: Path 20, Chesed–Tipharet
Element: Earth
Hebrew: Yod

The tenth trump represents chance and fate. The word "Tarot" can be interpreted as "wheel" or "cycle"; the trumps begin with 1 and end with 1. Rota is Latin for "wheel." The word appears on the tenth trump of the RWS version of this card and could be perceived as an anagram for Tarot. There have been many variations of this card but most versions involve an eight-spoked wheel as the focal device. The wheel's circular shape is eternal. Referring to the number of spokes astrologically, the eighth house encompasses the continuing cycle of life and death. The number "8," when laid on its side, becomes the glyph representing eternity. The number ten is the cyclic number of karmic completion and rebirth. Gnostic Christianity and later Catharism embraced the concept of karma and reincarnation despite the attempt made by the Roman Catholic Church to suppress it. Oddly, half of 10=5; the fifth trump is The Pope, The Pope plus the Wheel =15, the Devil, surely a Catharist viewpoint.

The number ten can be reduced to one: 1+0 =1. The first numbered trump is The Magician, which relates directly to the Wheel of Fortune as the magus tempts fate in order to create something out of nothing or alter the current of events. The Magician creates his own destiny through his actions, the crux of karmic philosophy. The two numbers present on the tenth trump, ten and eight, when combined equal eighteen—The Moon card of imagination and dreams.

Ten in its reduced form of one typifies the ruling Hebraic Yod. One is the number from which all numbers emanate as Yod is the Hebrew letter from which all others of the Hebrew alphabet evolve. Both are numbers of manifestation, reminding that one must manifest one's own good fortune. The Cabalistic path upon which The Wheel turns is the twentieth path, Consciousness of Will, vital to the individual, to the magician that dwells within manifesting one's own destiny.

The celestial influence of Virgo (ruled by Raphael, the archangel of chance and manifestation) permeates this tenth trump. Virgo seeks out naturally repeating patterns, waiting to bring about birth and rebirth in a Karmic cycle. Virgo is a positive sign that embodies service for the greater good, actions which guarantee progressive Karmic return.

Keywords

Time to take a risk, positive chance occurrence, take advantage of opportunities. New adventures present themselves. Unexpected good fortune, fate brings about success.

Strength XI

"I am not afraid, I was born to do this."

—Joan of Arc

The Maid of Orléans was born 1412 in the northeastern French village of Domrémy, the daughter of Jacques d'Arc and Isabelle Romée. Joan began receiving visions at age twelve of saints instructing her to deliver France from English domination and support the uncrowned Dauphin Charles VII. Some years later, the sovereign dispatched Joan to the siege of Orléans as part of a relief mission. She gained prominence after the siege was lifted in only nine days. Her subsequent victories led to Charles' coronation at Reims. In 1430, she was captured at Compiegne by English-allied Burgundians and put on trial by the pro-English Bishop Pierre Cauchon. Joan of Arc was burned at the stake in Rouen on May 30, 1431, for heresy when she was nineteen years old. Twenty-five years later, an inquisitorial court pronounced her innocent and declared her a martyr. Joan was beatified in 1909 and canonized in 1920, her feast day appropriately May 30.

Today's patron saint of France was the heroine of the Hundred Years' War. It is purported the Maid of Orleans also was a member of the Priory of Sion and clandestine blood relation to the French Capetian Dynasty. In *Inside the Priory of Sion,* Robert Howells states "The tradition of removing a bloodline child and placing it in the care of others to protect the lineage is seen in the early lives of both Moses and Joan of Arc." The war, a struggle for the French throne and territories, was primarily between two "bloodline" dynasties that trace their roots to the Merovingians: the Capetian House of Anjou and its English branch, the Plantagenets. The conflict was allegedly backed by opposing sides of the Templar/Sion schism. Early Angevins were closely associated with the Templar crusade and had acquired the Kingdom of Jerusalem. Later dynastic Angevins do not seem likely to have placed a simple peasant girl in a position that created profoundly significant political and religious ramifications. Was Joan of Arc a hereditary Angevin? Her given title of "Daughter of God" may allude to this theory. It is altogether possible that Joan was the bastard offspring of Louis II d'Anjou or the illegitimate daughter of Capetians Queen Isabeau and her brother-in-law, Louis of Orléans. Joan's famous banner bore two names "Jhesus–Maria"… perhaps referring to Jesus and Mary Magdalene.

Meaning

Archangel: Anael
Astrology: Venus
Cabala: Path 21, Chesed–Netsach
Element: Earth
Hebrew: Kaph

The eleventh trump, commonly known as Strength, has appeared as two distinct interpretations although there have been variants. Known originally as Fortitude, this Arcanum has been portrayed as a woman seated on a cubic throne breaking a pillar with her hands, a woman astride a golden lion, and a Herculean giant swinging a club at a lion at his feet.

Masonic and Golden Dawn lodges utilize reproductions of the two pillars of Solomon's Temple in their own designs. The broken pillar is significant as a metaphor: the left pillar of the Temple of Solomon was assigned the Hebrew appellation of Boaz. Boaz literally translates as "in strength." The left-most portion of the Cabalistic Tree of Life is the feminine pillar. Why is the pillar being broken and why is the lion subservient or overpowered, as in most renditions of this trump? The heraldic lion has been an armorial representative of many European royal houses, especially those of British origin. The lion is also the emblem of Jesus' familial tribe of Judah; Jesus was and is known as the Lion of Judah. Ancestrally speaking, Boaz and Ruth were the grandparents of Jesse whose descendants include Jesus himself.

The Marseilles decks and ensuing traditional decks lose the pillar completely. The woman is either opening or closing the standing lion's mouth. The RWS depicts a woman gently closing the lion's mouth, continentals show the mouth as being forced open. In classic variants, the woman's right hand reaches from the left side of the card and is positioned atop the lion's nose. The Hebrew correspondence Kaph signifies the hand, literally referring to the palm of the hand. In traditional Strength cards it is the palm of the hand that is placed upon the snout of the lion.

The planetary influence of Venus is ruled by Archangel Anael and embodies the eleventh trump. The strength of Love endures above all else. Goddess archetypes associated with the planet Venus are Isis and Mary Magdalene. The master number 11 belongs to Strength, representing the courage to inspire others to their higher purpose. It is a number representing a new cycle but dependent on the wisdom learned during the previous cycle. The twenty-first path on the Tree of Life is one of desire, coinciding with the planetary influence of Venus.

Keywords	Force of will, victory triumphs above overwhelming odds. Spiritual, moral, and intellectual fortitude. Endurance, determination, resilience. Control, compassion, ability.

The Hanged Man XII

"God wills it!"

—Templar Grand Master Gerard de Ridefort

Was the tenth Grand Master of the Knights Templar, Girard de Ridefort, a saint or sinner?

As history relates, the Cutting of the Elm was the result of an altercation between the Kings of France and England in 1188, during which a significant elm tree in the Champ Sacré near Gisors was felled. The tree marked the traditional field of Franco-Norman negotiations, as the location was situated on the border between English Normandy and the remaining dotminion of the French King. The tree was reported to be a huge growth, 800 years old, offering the only shade from unrelenting solar heat. Accounts narrate the meeting between Henry II of England and Philip II Augustus of France, in 1188, following the fall of Jerusalem. At Gisors, Henry II and his advisers stood under the elm tree while Philip and his entourage suffered in the full heat of the sun. After the meeting, Philip ordered the tree cut down and hacked to pieces, sending the message that he would offer no quarter to the English.

The year 1187 was not a good year for crusaders. That year saw Ridefort lead his meager troops into a disastrous battle for Jerusalem only to lose the holy city forever to the Seljuk, Saladin. Some say Ridefort feared being viewed as a coward, other accounts infer a gargantuan ego, other versions of the bitter tale recount stories of a man who truly believed he was doing God's work. Many of Ridefort's associates viewed this failed battle as a treasonous act. The catastrophic consequences resulted in the loss of the abbey mount, forcing the Order of Sion to move back to France to their new headquarters in Orleans. It is said the Cutting of the Elm the following year later was actually a physical metaphor graphically illustrating the Priory severing all ties with the Knights Templar.

Given existing evidence, an odd occurrence did happen at the field in Gisors in 1188. Whether or not it involved a dispute concerning two kings or the permanent separation between an order and its protégées will never be known, but an elm tree was felled possibly for allegorical reasons that won't find their way into the pages of accepted history. Existing accounts are scant and vague; perhaps the elm tree is concealing an affair of much greater significance.

Meaning

Archangel: Anael
Astrology: Libra
Cabala: Path 22, Geburah–Tipharet
Element: Air
Hebrew: Lamed

The twelfth trump has maintained uniformity throughout the centuries, displaying a male figure suspended by his leg from one tree with a cross-beam limb forming a Tau or three trees stylized as gallows; the leg positioning takes the shape of an inverted number 4. The Hanged Man changed when he crossed the English Channel from Europe to England. Continental decks display a figure hanging from a crossbeam supported by two trees, dangling by his left leg. The RWS reversed the suspended leg to the right and hung the hapless fellow from a single tree and crossbeam. Waite also added an aureole, scripting a message of martyrdom.

The numbers three, four, and twelve are significant in this card, linking the Hanged Man with the Knights Templar. Examining the continental versions, three trees are observed as is an inverted number four. The Hanged Man is the twelfth trump: 3x4=12. The Empress and The Emperor are trumps three and four sequentially. Could they represent the Capetian dynasty that sent the Templars to their doom? As Grand Master Jacques de Molay roasted at the stake in 1314, he uttered a curse that found his two inquisitors, Pope Clement and King Phillip, dead within the year. Justice had been exacted. Trump Justice VIII: 12-4=8. Peter the Hermit was closely associated with the Knights and the First Crusade. The Hermit XIIII: 12-3=9. The Knights were accused of venerating the Baphomet, the horned head representing all that is evil. The Devil XV: 12+3=15. The Knights met a catastrophic end, their towers destroyed. The card of catastrophe is The Tower XVI: 12+4=16.

Libra lends the scales of justice to The Hanged Man, his saving grace. As the scales suspend in mid-air, The Hanged Man also dangles in his element Air. The Cabalistic twenty-second path is Faithful Consciousness which personifies the card's positive attributes. The Hebrew Lamed evolved from *lamad*, meaning to teach or learn. Lamed corresponds with Libra, the zodiacal sign personifying balance. The Hanged Man is in equilibrium as he is swinging neither left nor right but hanging in a perfectly straight line. The letter's literal meaning is "ox-goad" (cattle prod): it is the Creative Power that forever goads mankind's animal instincts towards higher consciousness.

Keywords

Mystical enlightenment, personal growth. Spiritual instruction, walking a path of divinity. Rejection of material concerns, surrender to a higher power, humility, sacrifice. Stagnation.

Death XIII

"Few, if any, priests have captivated generations of spiritual questers and treasure hunters as Fr. Bérenger Saunière. What he found in his dilapidated church, just over 100 years ago, remains one the most enduring and fascinating mysteries of our time."

—Andrew Gough, founder and editor of *The Heretic Magazine* and *Mindscape Magazine*

François Bérenger Saunière (1852–1917), born in Montazels, France, attended school at St. Louis in Limoux, then entered seminary in Carcassonne in 1874. He was ordained a Roman Catholic priest in 1879. Saunière spent a short time teaching at the Narbonne seminary in 1885, but due to his unruly nature disciplinary action ensued. The priest found himself the appointee of a tiny village of approximately 300 inhabitants. It is there the mystery and intrigue that are Rennes-le-Chateâu take root.

The unorthodox priest preached anti-republican sermons from the pulpit in his little church dedicated to Mary Magdalene, urging his parishioners to vote for the restoration of the French monarchy. Saunière was suspended by the French minister of religion for one year then reinstated at Rennes le Chateâu. Saunière took on the task of renovating his decaying church. It is said he found ancient encrypted parchments under the pulpit, documents which held heretical implications and referred to the Priory of Sion. It is said of Sion's many objectives was to restore the Merovingian monarchy to the French throne. This find led to excavations by Saunière in and around his church and whispers of buried treasure began to stir. Saunière met with Parisian ecclesiastic councils, decoding experts, the Louvre, and individuals that would be considered strange company for any priest. Saunière renovated his village, including his own home Villa Bethania and personal library, the Tour Magdala. He had come into enormous wealth but no one seemed to know why. He decorated his refurbished church in curious fashion. A stone demon greets tourists and church-goers as he struggles to support the baptismal stoop. Noticeably out of place in a house of worship, this baptismal stoop is one of many peculiarities feverishly adorning Saunière's beloved church. Many believe this colorful beast to be the key to persistent rumors of fabulous treasure or cryptic parchments buried deep within specific confines of the area. Will anyone ever know the secrets of Saunière? When day is done, the Pyrenees sun drops in the twilight sky. The tiny church rises to receive the Languedoc moon, which broods knowingly over the mysterious little town of Rennes-le-Chateau.

Meaning

Archangel: Azrael
Cabala: Path 23, Geburah–Hod
Element: Water
Hebrew: Mem

Philosophical and symbolic "death" is an integral metaphor within the mystical initiatory process. One needs to "die" and be re-born through ritual into a new mindset, shedding previous spiritual restrictions and opening oneself to enlightenment. Symbolism and allegory are the keys to understanding these rituals of mystical fraternities including Freemasonry where symbolic "death" is a cornerstone of their initiatic system. Imagery and metaphor are the means to appreciating the rituals that are exemplified by the symbolic death, burial, and resurrection of the candidate. In the case of Freemasonry, the initiate of the Master Mason degree is portraying the legend of Hiram Abif during a ritualistic drama illustrating the master architect's murder. The Hermetic Order of the Golden Dawn relies on rituals celebrating the legends of death and resurrection of the Egyptian god Osiris. The Rosicrucian Order is alchemical in nature; alchemy seeks to define the "transition" (death) of the lesser to become resurrected as the greater—the Great Work: turning base metals into gold symbolic of the manifestation of soul into pure spirit. The Martinist Orders aligned themselves with this model in their lodges of the late 1800s as early Martinist philosophers were heavily influenced by the Order of the Rosy Cross.

Prior to the Marseilles decks, trump XIII had no zodiacal attribute, possibly a metaphysical reference to the nature of death itself. Its element was Water; this element was retained by the application of Scorpio to the Death card by the Victorian mystery schools. Other variations, including the Marseilles, Pierre Piobb, and Balbi ascribe the planetary influence of Saturn whose own glyph represents Saturn's sickle or scythe. Interpreting the actual meaning of the Death card as renewal and rebirth, the elemental influence of Water is apparent in its physical as well as baptismal implications. The appointment of the Hebrew letter Mem is significant in that Mem is the second of the three mother letters, signifying the Mother as the great Water of Life out of which all existance is born. Mem is the primordial sea which gives birth to all life. In Cabala, Mem signifies water, symbolizing the wellspring of the Torah and Talmud, the birth of knowledge and wisdom. This trump is ruled by Archangel Azrael—the Angel of Death.

Keywords	The end of a cycle, regeneration. Renewal, transformation, rebirth. New ideas, physical change. Release of old habits and ideas. Realization of mortality, acceptance of the unavoidable.

Temperance XIIII

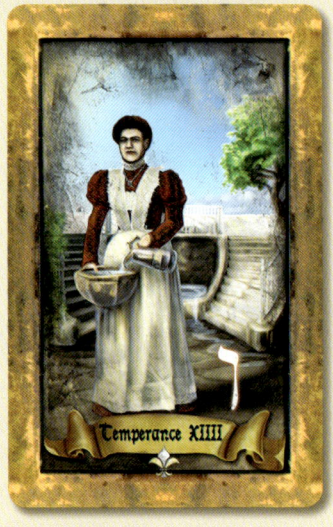

"You are walking on gold."

—Marie Dénarnaud (1868–1953)

In 1891, Marie Dénarnaud began working in Rennes-le-Château for Abbé Bérenger Saunière as a housekeeper and continued in this capacity of lifelong faithful servitude for twenty-one years. Some say she was specifically hand-picked by the Priory of Sion for this position of confidence. Besides attending to the duties of the house and its upkeep, Marie also served as the priest's banker, confidant, secretary, and rumors of a love tryst between the two were not uncommon but remain unfounded. The housekeeper shared Saunière's life and secrets. The villagers called her the priest's "Madonna" because in a few years within the cleric's employ, Marie began to stroll about the village adorned in fine jewelry and clothing. According to some, the priest became seriously ill January 12, 1917; but according to villagers, at that time he enjoyed robust health for a man of sixty-five. Still on that day, it is documented Saunière's loyal maid ordered his coffin. On the following January 17, the village priest tragically suffered what would prove to be a fatal stroke. On January 22, Fr. Bérenger Saunière died.

Twenty-two is significant in that the number finds itself woven throughout Rennes-le-Château. There are twenty-two Major Arcana of the Tarot, an esoteric device Saunière would have been familiar with given the occult revival of the late 1800's. Twenty-two is the number of the Magdalene's feast day, July 22. The skull above the entry gate to the graveyard has twenty-two teeth. A total of twenty-two stairs lead from the bottom to the top floor of the Tour Magdala, which housed Saunière's library. The tower, which has twenty-two battlements on top of it, is linked to the garden by twenty-two steps. The lone window in the Tour Magdala looks over a grotto known as the burial site of Mary Magdalene; the window is offset from the grotto by twenty-two degrees. The infamous Latin inscription over the doorway to Saunière's church dedicated to the Magdalene is purposely misspelled to number twenty-two letters. And finally, Marie Dénarnaud sold her master's estate, left to her in his will, to Noel Corbu on July 22, 1946. Saunière was twenty-two when he entered the seminary; interestingly, Marie was twenty-three when she embarked on her twenty-one year career, the two numbers that embrace twenty-two.

Meaning

Archangel: Samael
Astrology: Scorpio
Cabala: Path 24, Netzach-Tipharet
Element: Water
Hebrew: Nun

Temperance appears in the sequence of trumps as the last of three cards of personal virtue. The absence of Prudence is apparent. Included in traditional decks are Justice, Temperance, and Strength. The cardinal virtue, Prudence, is nowhere to be found; that is itself a mystery. A possible explanation may lie in the eulogy for nobleman Gian Galeazzo Visconti, written by Petrus de Castelleto in 1402. De Castello compares Visconti to "Twelve Stars which are twelve virtues." The sermon proposes a particular virtue and continues to describe how the deceased epitomized it. De Castello divides the virtues into four sets of three: Faith, Hope, Charity/Justice, Fortitude, Temperance/Prudence, Piety, Mercy/Magnificence, Intelligence, Humility. The second set contains three virtues found in Tarot; Prudence belongs to a different set of three.

The ruling zodiac of Scorpio is represented by different presentations of Temperance. Most familiar is the winged angelic figure pouring water from one container into another. Earlier interpretations of Temperance depict a seated woman gazing into a mirror with one hand whilst wrangling a snake with the other. Scorpio is a triune: the Eagle, the Snake, and the Scorpion. The angel's wings demonstrate the Eagle's wings upon which one may soar. Scorpio's watery nature is under control, tempered, as it is poured from one cup to the other. In earlier cards, Scorpio the Snake is taken under restraint—vanity and ego—as the woman gazes into her hand mirror. The snake is also biblical: temptation and the quest for knowledge at any cost. The Hebraic attribute of Nun means "fish," an animal that requires perfect stasis in water to survive. Temperance walks the twenty-fourth of the Cabalistic Paths, the path of Imaginative Consciousness. It is called this because the path provides an appearance for all created apparitions, in a form harmoniously befitting their stature and nature—balance, moderation. An interesting note: John the Evangelist's tetramorph is the Eagle and he is most often depicted with a chalice and associated with the Beloved Apostle. Often, a snake is depicted slithering from his cup, alluding to his attempted poisoning at Ephesus. Temperance's ruling archangel, Samael, is known as the archangel of poison and associated with the snake.

Keywords

Adaption, restraint, reasonableness. Moderation, equilibrium. Sound management, sobriety, serenity, harmony. Discretion, caution, carefulness. Self-control, modification.

The Devil XV

> "People who cease to believe in God or goodness altogether still believe in the devil… Evil is always possible. And goodness is eternally difficult."
>
> —Anne Rice, *Interview With The Vampire*

The list of indictments brought by the church against the Templar Knights included heresies such as homosexuality, sodomy, denial of Christ, spitting and trampling on the cross, and various other assumed deviltry. One allegation remains a constant throughout the church's accusations. Substantiated by fact, it is that of, strangely enough—"head worship," or rather a specific head, the Baphomet. Many of the warrior monks who refused to submit under torture to the litany of alleged crimes did indeed admit to worshipping a head utilized in Templar rituals.

The origin of the word Baphomet is debated. It may be a French corruption of two Arabic words the Templars would have been familiar with: Mahomet (Mohamad) or bufihimat meaning "Father (source) of Understanding."

Rosicrucian and hermetician of renown, Eliphas Levi, later lent his own interpretation of Baphomet in the 1800s, which has evolved into the contemporary symbolism and philosophy, that of the goat-headed, hermaphroditic centaur-like creature, now a modern occult symbol and demiurge of choice for modern-day Satanists.

The identity of the head worshipped by the Templars remains an enigma, but descriptions exist. During the arrests of 1307, a silver reliquary in the shape of a woman's head was confiscated, inside of which two head bones were wrapped in red and white cloth (Templar colors). The relic bore a label which read "Caput LVIIIm": Head 58m. The number may have designated the relic as one in a series and "m" may have been the astrological symbol for Virgo. Other accounts attest to the head as having been male bearing a white, red, or dark beard. Interestingly, the name "Baphomet" can also be interpreted as "Baptist of Wisdom," a title that could appropriately apply to the Knights' bearded patron saint, John the Baptist, who was believed to be a Gnostic. After John's beheading ordered by Herod at the behest of Salomé, the Baptist was revered for centuries by underground Gnostic cults called "Johannites." They believed John to be the true Messiah and Jesus a usurper. Theories exist declaring Templars observed this doctrine. This may explain many of the charges of heresy levied at the Templars, especially those accusations of denying Christ's divinity and defiling the cross.

Meaning

Archangel: Sachiel
Astrology: Sagittarius
Cabala: Path 25, Yesod-Tipharet
Element: Fire
Hebrew: Samekh

The Devil is often depicted as a goat-headed, centaur-like creature having both male and female characteristics. These hermaphroditic features typify two spheres on the Tree of Life—Tipharet, male ruled by the Sun, and Yesod, female ruled by the Moon. This fifteenth trump is directly related to The Lovers VI: 15=1+5=6. However, we find the lovers of the sixth trump have now become captives of their own shortcomings when imprisoned in The Devil card. The number 6 specifically relates to duty, love, service, marriage, and family, but The Devil can twist these virtues until they are unrecognizable.

This card is often interpreted as Baphomet, the goat-headed god that has long been a modern symbol of the "dark side" and a veneration of modern Satanism. This distinction owes itself to a bastardization of a misunderstood mysterious Templar ritual. The name Baphomet traces to the end of the Crusades. It is said the Knights worshipped a severed head, the Baphomet, the identity of which remains an enigma, but legend suggests the patron saint of the Templars, John the Baptist. Eliphas Levi, later lent his own interpretation of Baphomet, which has evolved into the current symbolism. Recognized as a foreboding card, The Devil is more a warning of personal weakness than forces of surrounding evil. This card counsels to bear responsibility for actions. In The Devil, matter has dominated over spirit; humankind is reduced to its baser instincts.

The Hebrew letter associated with The Devil XV is Samekh, which is shaped liked an archer's bow. Samekh is the equivalent of the English "S"—the hissing of the snake coiled in the Tree of Knowledge. The Devil trods the twenty-fifth Cabalistic path, the Testing of Consciousness, daring one to resist temptation. This way of wrath is charged with positive/negative energies, thus the physical male and female characteristics. Sagittarius is the zodiacal attribute of the fifteenth trump, ruled by Archangel Sachiel, lord of material gain. The Devil's tail has been depicted as resembling the Archer's arrow. This Fire sign seeks knowledge on the tree of forbidden fruit at the risk of its weaknesses. Although intellectual and philosophical, Sagittarians can be superficial, restless and irresponsible, giving in to impulse, ego, and dependency.

Keywords

Success at any cost, greed. Refusing to see the truth. Addiction, over-indulgence, sexual gratification, materialism. A need for pleasure. Bondage, disregard, false pride. Health issues.

The Tower XVI

"Kill them all. God will know his own."

—The Abbot Arnaud Amaury, 1209, the battle at Beziers, the first and bloodiest combat of the Albigensian Crusade

The Cathar fortress of Montségur was perched atop a mountain of the same name. Rising a precarious 3,000 feet above the Languedoc region of southern France, the massive battlement was last to fall during the final throes of an unimaginable genocide perpetrated by brutal armies dedicated to the pope and the French king. The Albigensian Crusade crushed the peaceable Cathar society, an ancient religious sect thriving primarily in southern France, declared heretical for a multiplicity of reasons. The dualist Cathars renounced Trinitarian dogma, denied the concept of Jesus' divinity, and maintained the Christ was fully immersed in the human experience including taking a wife (as was required of all kings and rabbis of ancient Judaic tradition). This bride was the much maligned Mary Magdalene. Ironically, the Cathar beliefs were closer the tenets of ancient Christianity than those of the Roman Church.

During an annihilation lasting almost fifty years (1209 –1255), papal troops launched from the northern fortress of Citeaux marched south, devastating Cathar cities and villages. It is known Templar Knights fought on both behalf of the church *and* the Cathars as many of the order, including the fourth Grand Master Bertrand de Blanchefort, hailed from the Languedoc region. Evidence shows the Templars and the Cathars were actually strongly allied. In 1243, Montségur was besieged by legions of Catholic loyalists. The inhabitants of the castle finally surrendered in March 1244 after a mêlée lasting ten months. The Cathar faithful and their Templar defenders were eventually roasted en masse in a bonfire blazing on the grounds of the fortress.

Rumor holds five Cathar prefects managed to escape the ensuing holocaust. Aided by surviving Templars, they carried with them a mysterious "treasure" of which there has been much speculation: the Cathar treasury, esoteric books, documents and genealogies, or possibly the actual cup known as the holy grail. Rome certainly wanted to take possession of these artifacts as they could have proven to be quite counter-productive to Vatican interests, possibly heralding the downfall of the Mother Church. One school of thought maintains this cache was secreted out of France via Templar ships and may have found a clandestine home in Scotland.

Meaning

Archangel: Cassiel
Astrology: Capricorn
Cabala: Path 26, Hod-Tipharet
Element: Earth
Hebrew: Ayin

Arcanum XVI may reference the Tower of Babel. Built after the Great Flood by the Babylonians, the edifice was constructed to facilitate man's ascent to heaven. Following the flood, few human beings remained: "And the whole earth was of one language, and of one speech." God destroyed the Tower, scattered all peoples, and "confounded the language of all the earth," producing different races and dialects. This scenario is associated with destruction and catastrophe, common interpretations of The Tower card, but may also be construed as regeneration. These divine acts may represent the seeding of the earth, producing the richness of diversity. Instead of inflicting punishment, God may have actually exercised a strategy.

The Tower from a Priory perspective offers a different viewpoint. Tales promote a powerful secret society protecting and sponsoring a hidden royal bloodline. Aramaic was Jesus' own native tongue. A direct connection of The Tower to Mary Magdalene can be found by way of the Aramaic translation of *magdala*—"tower." The Tower may be conveying the destruction of the royal House of David and its heirs by the twenty-year military campaign initiated by Pope Innocent III in 1209, a genocide sanctioned by the Mother Church. The general appearance of The Tower card is most often associated with the Marseilles Tarot, therefore this particular card must have been of some significance. With its toppling crown, flames, and thunderbolt one could assume this is a representation of the Cathar stronghold of Montségur and the decimation of a royal bloodline. Path 26 on the Tree of Life is that of Renewed Consciousness; that which is destroyed is, in a sense, purified and must be rebuilt. The Hebraic correspondence of Ayin signifies two eyes: utilizing the perception of good or evil, optimism or pessimism, and spiritual sight. The eyes constantly produce water, the universal purifier necessary for cleansing and renewal. Archangel Cassiel lords over The Tower; he can be perceived as an upsetting and challenging influence. The astrological attribute of Capricorn denotes change may be difficult to achieve. The symbolism teaches that no matter how much status one achieves, spiritual enlightenment will remain elusive until the bonds of attachments to the material are broken.

Keywords	Emergence of that which was imprisoned, a residential move, a significant separation or expulsion. Rupture, overthrow. Calamity, catastrophe, destruction, decay followed by renewal.

The Star XVII

"I've always preferred mythology to history. History is truth that becomes an illusion. Mythology is an illusion that becomes reality."

—Jean Cocteau (1889–1963)

Jean Maurice Eugène Clément Cocteau was a prolific French artist of renown: poet, novelist, dramatist, designer, playwright, painter, and filmmaker. Cocteau is best known for his novel *Les Enfants Terribles* (1929), and the films *Blood of a Poet* (1930), *Les Parents Terribles* (1948), *Beauty and the Beast* (1946), and *Orpheus* (1949).

Born near Paris to an aristocratic family, the intensely religious Cocteau enjoyed a certain notoriety within the bohemian circles in which he thrived, impressing the intellectual community with the brilliance of his work. As his reputation evolved, he was patronized by some of Europe's most respected nobility. By the latter part of his life, he had been elected to the prestigious Academie Francaise, inducted with a ceremonial sword designed by Picasso.

Cocteau earned the title "Poet of the Year," was made a "Chevalier of the Legion of Honor," and was invited to Oxford to receive an honorary Doctor of Letters. And, according to the *Dossiers Secrets*, the poet/novelist/filmmaker/artist—and opium addict—was also the twenty-sixth Grand Master of the Priory of Sion.

Cocteau had connections to individuals purported to be Priory members or Grand Masters such as Victor Hugo and Claude Debussy. The artist upheld a life-long admiration for Leonardo da Vinci and referred to the Renaissance genius often, resulting in his theory regarding the use of line in his artwork. In this way, Cocteau adopted his approach executing the transmission of esoteric secrets using sacred geometry and symbolism. Indeed, some of his more mysterious work may have actually been commissioned by Sion. The Priory holds special reverence for the biblical figure of Mary Magdalene both as the mother of Christ's children and as an embodiment of the Venus/Isis goddess archetype. Cocteau also seemed to bear a similar reverence for this woman. William Emboden, who has written extensively on Cocteau, says Cocteau spoke of a mystical effluvium of the Madeleine Church in Paris, like the emanations from some antique temple that held him to the region of that edifice. Surely Cocteau, despite shortcomings, embodied philosophies esteemed by the Priory of Sion.

Meaning

Archangel: Anael
Astrology: Mercury
Cabala: Path 27, Netzach-Hod
Element: Air
Hebrew: Peh

Traditionally, a nude woman appears on The Star XVII dispensing water into a stream and onto the ground from two different pitchers. This could be interpreted as the Water Bearer, symbolizing the new Age of Aquarius, pouring the waters of spirit and truth heralding a future time when the mysteries of the Priory unfold. She kneels beneath an eight-pointed star surrounded by seven more stars representing the Pleiades venerated by the ancients as signifying fertility and hope. This totals eight stars present on the card. Every eight years, Venus glides through the heavenly Pleiades mapping out a fairly precise pentacle. The pentagram, a symbol of the Sacred Feminine, has been erroneously associated with evil as part of a centuries-long campaign by Catholic doctrine to discriminate against women within the church. The Star card is the seventeenth card of the Major Arcana: 1+7=8. Mary Magdalene is traditionally associated with the planet Venus and she is first mentioned in the New Testament in Luke, chapter eight. Babylonian goddess Ishtar was envisioned as a deity associated with the planet Venus, the "eight-pointed star." Interestingly, the transit of the card's ruling planet of Mercury from Venus lasts eight hours. Traditionally, the larger star present on this card is said to represent transcendence. It seems apparent The Star was intended to illustrate this planetary phenomenon.

The Star's ruling archangel Anael is associated with the planet Venus. The Hebrew letter related with The Star, Peh, literally means mouth, but is also synonymous with expression or awakening. The Star's astrological correspondence, Mercury, is a heavenly body which represents, among other things, speech which coincides with Peh's literal meaning. The keyword for Mercury is "communicate"; humans consistently utilize articulation and discourse. This use of language implies reason, the one characteristic that separates mankind from the "lower" animals, thus implying ascendency—the god-like ability to reach for the stars. Path 27 on the Tree of Life, the road to the Sun, is called the path of Profound Intelligence, which is integral to experiencing the enlightenment offered by The Star, when Venus greets her Seven Sisters as a fervent symbol of hope, healing, enlightenment, prosperity, and fertility.

Keywords

Potential, inspiration. Promising portents, favorable currents, excellent prospects, true destiny. Achievement, improved health. Illumination, clarification. Intellectual fulfillment.

The Moon XVIII

"And there were certain men, who were defiled by the dead body of a man, that they could not keep the Passover on that day: and they came before Moses and before Aaron on that day."

—The Bible, Numbers, 9:6

The Church of St. Mary Magdalene in Rennes-le-Château, France, lies at the heart of the Priory mysteries. Refurbished and meticulously redecorated by the village priest Abbé Saunière in the late 1800s, the church's interior décor could easily be described as eccentric. Odd statues stand ever vigilant on their pedestals throughout the church; many say these effigies hold clues to unraveling the secrecies of Rennes-le-Château. To be sure, even the Stations of the Cross are not without their peculiarities.

The Way of the Cross in the Church of St. Mary Magdalene was installed in 1897, ordered out of a catalogue from Giscard in Toulouse. These stations, bas relief painted under Saunière's direction, have been cause for endless speculation among researchers as many of the stations' details appear to be quite compelling. Firstly, the stations were hung upon the church walls sequencing in the opposite direction than those traditionally hung in Catholic churches. Quirks abound: all the stations in this particular sanctuary bear the Masonic Rose-Croix in their framework, a golden griffin appears in Station I, a golden helmet and ladder seem out of place on Station II, Station VIII shows a brutalized Jesus staring down at a woman and her small child who is wrapped in a Scottish tartan blanket. However, probably no other station in this series is as enigmatic as the final Station XIV, which traditionally shows Jesus' corpse being carried into his tomb by Joseph of Arimathea and Nicodemus. In Saunière's rendition there are startling differences. It is known Jesus died on a specific Friday afternoon—14 Nisan, the Day of Preparation for oncoming Passover beginning in the evening after sunset. The Sabbath day also begins Friday evenings a few minutes before sunset. Saunière's version of Station XIV clearly shows a night-time sky with full moon. Joseph and Nicodemus are moving the body of Jesus. This scenario would have been impossible as Jewish law strictly forbade the handling of a dead human body during Passover and on the Sabbath. These laws continue within the orthodox Jewish community. The men also appear to be stepping out of the tomb, not into it. The conclusion is obvious yet disturbing: there was no corpse, the supposed dead man was still alive.

Meaning

Archangel: Uriel
Astrology: Aquarius
Cabala: Path 28, Netzach-Yesod
Element: Air
Hebrew: Tzaddi

The Moon XVIII appears to have been rendered in four distinct fashions. Prior to the Marseille variants, The Moon was illustrated three ways. The Visconti family of cards portrays a young barefoot maiden clothed in the attire of a working class woman. She holds aloft a crescent moon in her right hand and in her left, she holds the ends of her rope drawstring. The Minchiate Moon card depicts an astrologer sitting under the moon, a compass resembling a

"V" in his raised right hand. The Gringonneur/Charles VI/Estensi deck shows two astronomers/astrologers creating furtive calculations in a journal by the light of a crescent moon, each holds a compass device in their right hands; the astronomer on the left holds his upward, opened in a "V" shape. The one on the right holds his device downward on the right page in the book, the compass opened in an "Λ" shape. This particular card went through a metamorphosis when expressed through the Tarot of Marseille. This is the image that has withstood the test of Tarot time and has remained entrenched within the Tarot dynamic with different variations depending on the deck's theme. The maiden disappeared as had the astronomers/astrologers. Found in their places are two castle towers and a glowing moon above two baying canines, one a wild wolf and one a domestic dog. The full moon bears a human face reflecting the sun as its rays release Yod-like drops. A crayfish appears in the stream, at the beginning of the path leading between the canines and towers, possibly representing mankind's primordial origins. The dog and wolf graphically symbolize the inherent nature of the logical and instinctive aspects of the human mind.

Archangel Uriel rules The Moon, presiding over all that is unexpected, good and bad. Cabalistic Path 28 is one of Natural Intelligence. The Hebrew correspondence of Tzaddi means "fish-hook," which derives from its root word meaning "to capture." In light of The Moon's implications and the presence of howling hounds, could this Hebraic reference suggest recapturing one's sanity? Aquarius, the Water Bearer, is an eccentric individual. Traditionally, those born under the sign of the Water Bearer are the unconventional and committed to interests out of the ordinary, making the sign of Aquarius an appropriate influence for The Moon card.

Keywords

Psychic ability, dark forces, mysterious meanings, hidden enemies.
The unknown, instinctive or irrational fears. Deception, illusion. Mental unrest, psychosis, paranoia. Intuition.

The Sun XVIIII

"No, Sir, his manners are such that he would not know how to ask a woman to accept his service, although his looks are of Love's color."

—Wolfram von Eschenbach (*Parzival*) 1170–1220

The Widow's Son is a pivotal character embraced by many secret societies but may take on different identities according to each fraternity's philosophies. According to Freemasonry, the master architect and builder of the sacred Temple, Hiram Abiff (the true founder of the fraternity according to Masonic canon), was the Widow's Son. He is referred to twice in scripture as being the son of a widow of the tribe of Naphtali. Another enduring legend of the Widow's Son is the epic poetry regarding a certain Welsh knight named Perceval (also spelled Percival, Percivale, Parzival, and Parsifal) and his quest for the holy grail. Scores of interpretations and scholarly accounts have endured through the centuries concerning the exploits of the Widow's Son whose father had been killed in a public tournament. Perceval's mother, Kamuellès, retreats to the forest to raise her only son. In due course, the young man is taken under the wing of Welsh King Arthur and awarded a seat at the Round Table of Knights where, through his exploits, Perceval becomes known as the Grail Knight. First penned by Welsh cleric Nennius in the ninth century, the legend of the chaste young knight blossomed through time in all directions, flourishing through various artistic mediums and secret societies. Chrétien de Troyes set the standard for Perceval epics with his unfinished *Perceval, le Conte du Graal*, written between the years 1181–1191. German knight and poet, Wolfram von Eschenbach, based his significant medieval classic *Parzival* (early 1200s) on Chrétien's work and likened the Knights of the Round Table to the Knights Templar. The Perceval epics are comprised primarily of two major themes: heroic acts of chivalry and courtly love, a source of inspiration for the troubadours. Wolfram began a prequel, Titurel (The Grail King), which was later continued by another writer. Robert de Boron, a French poet of the thirteenth century, continued the tradition with his works *Perceval, Joseph d'Arimathe*, and *Merlin*. Sir Thomas Malory, a Welsh or English knight of the fifteenth century, authored *Le Morte d'Arthur*, another famous account of the Grail Knight's adventures. *Perceval* is often accompanied by other knights of the court, most famously Sir Galahad, Sir Bors, and Sir Lancelot. Galahad, Perceval, and Bors are considered the three Grail Knights.

Meaning

Archangel: Sachiel
Astrology: Pisces
Cabala: Path 29, Malkuth-Netzach
Element: Water
Hebrew: Qoph

Interpreting this card as "The Son," the astrological and Hebraic correspondences are startlingly significant. Pisces, the iconic symbol of Jesus the Son/Sun God in both Christian and esoteric interpretations, has the archangelic correspondence of Sachiel who claims the celestial title "King of the Gods." The Hebrew name for Pisces' ruling planet, Jupiter (the Roman King of the Gods), is "Tzedek," which means righteousness and justice, the qualities of kings. The Egyptian names associated with Sachiel are Isis and Horus. The fruit associated with Sachiel are bunches of grapes—the vine, a standard metaphor representing the Davidic bloodline. The Sun's ruling Hebrew letter, Qoph, is associated with crowns and kings. It literally means "horizon," the exalted state of Aleph (associated with the Magician). In Isaiah 49:16, Jesus expresses concern for his kingdom; Jesus could certainly be seen as a magician king as his ancestor before him, King Solomon. Of particular interest, the ancient Hebrew Qoph was depicted as a circle bisected by a horizontal line: the Sun splitting the horizon. The 29th Path on the Tree of Life is that of The Physical Intelligence. It is called this because it represents the growth of all things that become physical on Earth under the Sun.

Following this thread of thought, Freemasonry asserts the title "The Widow's Son" is applied to Hiram Abiff (the architect of the Temple of Solomon). It is written in the first Book of Kings, there was "a widow's son of the tribe of Naphtali." Modern Freemasonry has adopted this tradition with varying interpretations. Some lodges refer to themselves as The Widow's Sons in alliance with the Master Masons who took care of Hiram's mother after the architect was murdered by three ruffians for not divulging esoteric secrets of sacred geometry. Other Masonic chapters address themselves as Sons of the Widow, aligning themselves as sons of Hiram's widow. Supporters of the exiled House of Stuart claimed the Masonic title for themselves. These Jacobites sought to organize a system of political Freemasonry by which they hoped to secure the restoration of the House of Stuart to the throne of England. They transferred the tradition of Hiram Abiff to Charles II, betrayed by his followers, and called him the Widow's Son. He was the son of Henrietta Maria of France, queen consort of England, Ireland, Scotland, and the widow of executed King Charles Stuart I.

Keywords

Success, attainment, achievement. Health and vivacity. Vibrancy, happiness, energy, attunement. Self-assurance, talent, confidence. Positive growth—business or personal.

Judgement XX

"Your venerable stupidness may know, that
we are nobody's vassal in temporal matters."

—Philip IV, King of France

Philip IV (1268–1314), called the Fair, was King of France from 1285 until his death. His marriage to Joan I of Navarre bestowed upon him the titles Philip I, King of Navarre and Count of Champagne from 1284 to 1305. Philip was instrumental in the transformation of France from a feudal country to a centralized state. The king ruled as an unchallenged monarchy with the ambition to place his kin on Europe's thrones. Princes from his house of Capet ruled in Naples and Hungary, however, he failed to place a Capet as Holy Roman Emperor.

Notable conflicts include a dispute with Edward I of England and the Avignon Papacy, but Philip IV is most infamous for the annihilation of the Order of the Knights Templar in 1307, which coincidentally followed his expulsion of French Jewry in 1306. The king was intensely eager to rid his lands of Templars, most of whom at this point had commanderies headquartered in France and answered to no one.

King Philip was deeply indebted to the Knights, having borrowed heavily from them. He was humiliated when, fleeing a Parisian mob, he was forced to seek refuge in a Templar preceptory. Further adding to the indignation, the king was arrogantly rejected when he himself applied for membership to the order as a postulant. Philip desperately desired the Templar wealth and power. The answer was simple: to align himself with the papacy as papal patience was growing thin with the increasingly independent Templar state. Philip and his ministers engineered the deaths of two successive Italian popes, securing the election of a French bishop to the papal throne which was then moved to Avignon. The new pontiff, Clement V, realized his debt to the king and could hardly refuse his demands, primarily the dismantling of the Knights Templar. In October 1307, on Friday 13, a papal bull was issued demanding the arrest of all Templars on trumped up charges of heresy. The result was the enmasse torture and death of the Templar Knights. As the last Grand Master, Jacques De Molay, roasted alive he uttered a curse: "Let evil swiftly befall those who have wrongly condemned us! God will avenge our death!" Both Pope Clement V and King Philip the Fair were dead within a year of De Molay's demise.

Meaning

Archangel: Cassiel
Astrology: Saturn
Cabala: Path 30, Yesod-Hod
Element: Earth
Hebrew: Resh

Since the early Tarots, this trump has depicted what many interpret to be the second coming. Angelic beings blast trumpets heralding the Day of Judgement, and what appear to be human corpses rise from their tombs, arms raised in acceptance of their fate before God. The trumpets are traditionally adorned with a type of banner, standard, or white flag bearing a red cross closely resembling the Templar emblem, as seen in both the Marseille and Victorian versions of this card. The dead also appear to be emerging from the waters in the background; this may be a reference to the sea giving up its dead on the Day of Judgement, as described in the Book of Revelation.

Mystery schools judge the candidates seeking initiation. Applicants may attend open-house meetings, answer advertisements, or simply ask to join. The process varies among various lodges and chapters. It is the aspirant's obligation to ask to join; candidates may be encouraged to ask, but they are never invited. Formalities follow to judge a candidate's suitability. Being called to "rise from the dead" is a symbolic reference to the aspirants' journey to enlightenment, shedding the "death" of the ashes of ignorance and rising like the phoenix to spiritual awakening.

Judgement is ruled by the Hebrew Resh—the thinker and power of creative thought. It is no wonder this letter's literal meaning is "the head." It is representative of man's final unfoldment. Archangel Cassiel returns to remind that perseverance overcomes adversity. The path on the Tree of Life ruling Judgment is the 30th Path—the Path of Collective Consciousness. This tells us Judgement symbolizes karmic lessons and the return of past energies. This is the opportunity for rebirth and renewal; put judgment aside and instead be guided by love and forgiveness. Saturn is the twentieth trump's ruling planet and applies a literal meaning to the Judgement card. In astrology, Saturn is associated with restriction and limitation, rules and regulations. Saturn brings structure and meaning, representing boundaries, responsibilities, and commitments. It brings definition to life and an awareness of the need for self-control. Similarly, Saturn's lessons actually promote psychological growth by encouraging stability.

Keywords

Renewal, karmic completion. Conclusions, results, outcomes. Answers to questions, end of doubt, final decisions. Significant news, important announcements. Life change, regeneration.

The World XXI

*"Apart from a few admirable drawings,
they do not reveal this or that side of nature, but
develop themes under a sublime register…"*

—*Réflexion sur Poussin* (*Thinking about Poussin*)
Avogdor Arikha 1929

The sublime genius of classic art offers the casual admirer dramatic beauty of tempera, oil ,and water put to canvas, wood, and stone. To the trained eye of an esoterist, these works are allegories composed of myriad clues alluding to philosophies considered heretical by Mother Church. Artists such as Leonardo, Michelangelo, Raphael, Botticelli, Dürer, Bosch, van Eyck, and Teniers were masters of hidden meaning. By employing sacred geometry, camouflaged symbolism, and optical tricks these masters conveyed ancient truths to those with eyes to see without rousing the suspicion of the church.

Perhaps no other painting has prompted enthusiasm among members of secret societies, treasure hunters, esoterists, and Rennes-le-Château aficionados as Poussin's masterpiece *Les Bergers d'Arcadie* also known as *Et In Arcadia Ego*. Two versions of this enigmatic piece were painted during the years 1594–1665 by master artist Nicholas Poussin. They are bucolic paintings portraying shepherds from antiquity, however, the three men appear intensely concerned about a stone tomb, one they have apparently stumbled upon in the countryside. They are accompanied by a red-haired woman who seems to be pregnant. The later version is the most famous account of the subject, hanging in the Louvre museum in Paris under the name *Les Bergers d'Arcadie* ("The Arcadian Shepherds"). Forever linked with the legends of Rennes-le Château, scores of books have been written chronicling this painting, meticulously surveying the sacred geometry contained within it and the story presented. Special interest are the words chiseled into the tomb: *Et In Arcadia Ego*. This simple phrase is the stuff of legendary debate among the genre's dedicated researchers. It is a Latin idiom said to interpret several ways: "And I am in Arcadia," "I was also in Arcadia," and "I am dead in Arcadia" are some of the versions. A stone replica of this painting, known as the *Shepherd's Monument*, is to be found on the grounds of Shugborough Manor in Staffordshire, England, home to the noble family of Litchfield, cousins of Queen Elizabeth II. The image is an exact copy of the original, however, it appears reversed. Etched in its base is a strange coded inscription which today remains unsolved: D.O.U.O.S.V.A.V.V.

Meaning

Archangel: Sachiel
Astrology: Jupiter
Cabala: Path 31, Malkuth-Hod
Element: Fire
Hebrew: Tav

The World XXI traditionally heralds the completion of the Tarot sequence, depending on the placement of The Fool card within the Major Arcana sequence. The World may actually be the twenty-second card should The Fool begin the Majors or appear after Judgment in the twenty-first position. If tTe Fool is placed as the final card, The World maintains her twenty-first designation. According to R. Allendy, this number "contains the ratios of the principle of individuality 1 with the cosmic differentiation 20. These ratios would constitute an act of organization: 2 + 1 = 3. Thus the principle of individuality, placed between the world of the spirit and that the matter, realizes in itself the meeting of both."

Traditionally, this trump depicts a nude woman in the center of a vesica piscis-shaped green wreath, gathered and bound by crossed red ribbon, surrounded by the Four Tetramorphs. Throughout Europe, images of Jesus surrounded by the Four Tetramorphs can be seen chiseled into the ancient stonework of Gothic cathedrals, gracing covers of scripture, and portraiture of medieval art. The tetramorphs are four angelic beings conceived from earlier Babylonian symbolism representing the four fixed signs of the zodiac: Lion (Leo), Ox (Taurus), Man/Water-bearer (Aquarius), and Eagle (Scorpio). They likewise symbolize the four alchemical elements of Fire, Earth, Air, and Water. Gnostic Christians applied this ancient zodiacal symbolism to the authors of the four gospels: Mark, Luke, Matthew, and John. The Marseille Tarots adopted this imagery but replaced the central figure of Christ with a nude woman depicted in the center of this most feminine of sacred geometric forms. For the ancients, she was Sophia—Wisdom. She is the Holy Spirit, the triple Goddess: maiden, matron, crone, and all the pivotal Marys of the New Testament. She is the Goddess, equal consort to the Divine.

Path 32 is called the Serving or Worshipped consciousness because it directs the motion of the seven planets, each in its own proper course. The rulers Archangel Sachiel (King of the Angels) and Jupiter (King of the Gods) are concerned with expansion, proliferation, and propagation—qualities necessary for a world to thrive.

Keywords

Renewal, karmic completion. Conclusions, results, outcomes. Answers to questions, end of doubt, final decisions. Significant news, important announcements. Life change, new paths.

Chapter Six

The Minor Arcana

Cups
The Rosicrucians

Today's Rosicrucian Order (AMORC) is a distant echo from its original predecessor of the same name founded in late medieval Germany by Christian Rosenkreuz, although both maintain to adhere to a philosophy based on ancient esoteric truths that provide insight into the nature of the physical universe and the spiritual realm.

Exactly when the Rosicrucian Order came into existence is a matter of debate. One school of thought upholds the theory that, in 1188, the Priory of Sion and the Rosicrucian Order were the same, the latter being a subtitle for the clandestine fraternity. It is said Sion itself proclaims Rosicrucian orders to be its spiritual emissaries, allowing Sion a means by which it can influence society. Others place the origin of Rosicrucianism in late 1500s Germany, its forerunner being the secret society developed by brilliant heretical Dominican friar, Giordano Bruno. Bruno, an Italian fond of travel, put down roots in Germany where he laid the groundwork for his philosophical fraternity, the Giordanisti. Bruno believed ancient hermeticism to be the true Gnostic religion, however, his society was short lived due to the cleric's imprisonment by the Inquisition in 1592. It is about this time, between 1607 and 1616, two anonymous manifestos were published in Germany: the *Fama Fraternitatis RC* (*The Fame of the Brotherhood of RC*) and the *Confessio Fraternitatis* (*The Confession of the Brotherhood of RC*). The documents present an order of mystic philosophers promoting a "Universal Reformation of Mankind." The documents' influence gave rise to the "Rosicrucian Enlightenment," which spread quickly throughout Europe. Purported Priory of Sion Grand Master Robert Fludd (1574–1637) had a keen interest in Rosicrucian philosophy and may have been a member himself.

According to historian David Stevenson, the Order of the Rose Cross was also influential to Freemasonry as it was emerging in late 1500s Scotland. Scotland is often referred to as the birthplace of Freemasonry and the two societies are frequently compared. Over the years, many mystery schools and secret fraternities claim to have developed their principles, in whole or in part, based on the original Rosicrucian philosophy.

The Novice of Cups

*"Forthwith now to the mountain wend
whereon three stately Temples stand,
And there see all from end to end."*

—From *The Chymical Wedding of Christian Rosenkreuz* (1616)

Christian Rosenkreuz is the legendary, perhaps metaphorical, founder of the Rosicrucian Order. German born in 1378, the last of a noble family in poor circumstances, he was placed in a monastery at the age of four. As a young man, he set out on a pilgrimage to the Middle East where he studied and became well known for his medical skill. Then he traveled to Arabia where he was tutored in the hermetic sciences by mystics. After studying botany and zoology in Egypt and Cabala in Fez, Rosenkreuz was equipped to teach the erudite of Europe what he had learned. Rosenkreuz eventually returned to Germany where he assembled seven supporters. This band of eight founded the Fraternity of the Rose Cross with Christian Rosenkreuz (Frater C.R.C.) as Grand Master of the Order.

Three Rosicrucian manifestos, published anonymously in early seventeenth century Germany, introduce the order's founder as "Frater C.R.C." The first document is the *Fama Fraternitatis Rosae Crucis*, which appeared in 1614 followed in 1615 by the *Confessio Fraternitatis*. In 1616, the *Chymical Wedding of Christian Rosenkreuz* appeared in Strasbourg revealing for the first time the founder's name as Christian Rosenkreuz. The order appealed to Christians, especially Lutherans who held particular disdain for the papacy.

Legend conveys Rosenkreuz' body was discovered by a brother of the order in 1604 in a perfect state of preservation, almost one hundred-fifty years after his death, which occurred in secrecy within the heptagonal chamber erected by Rosenkreuz as a storehouse of knowledge. Rumor has it Rosenkreuz' tomb is inscribed with the words "*Jesus mihi omnia, nequaquam vacuum, libertas evangelii, dei intacta gloria, legis jugum*" ("Jesus is everything to me, by no means empty, the freedom of the gospel, the untouched glory of god, the yoke of the law"), attesting to the founder's religious convictions. Rosenkreuz' crypt, according to the description presented in the legend, appears to be located in interior parts of the Earth, recalling the alchemical motto V.I.T.R.I.O.L.: "*Visita Interiora Terrae Rectificando Invenies Occultum Lapidem* ("Visit the Interior Parts of the Earth; by Rectification Thou Shalt Find the Hidden Stone").

NATURE: Dreaming the Dream
ELEMENT: Earth of Water
TETRAGRAMMATON: Heh
CARD PERSONAGE:
This card represents a young child, adolescent, or teenager of either sex, possessed of light to medium brown hair, light to medium complexion and brown eyes.

keywords

Romantic opportunities. Dreams, sensitivity, idealism, and compassion. Spirituality, charisma, and poise. News regarding love, engagement, marriage, pregnancy, or birth.

If the Novice of Cups represents a person: An artist, writer, poet, psychic, counselor, or clergyperson. A chef, an actor, or a sculptor. An admirer of the theatre, cinema, or humanities.

The Initiate of Cups

*"A man who knows everything
and who never dies."*

—Voltaire

The Count of Saint-Germain (1712–1784), was the purported Grand Master of the Priory of Sion during the mid 1700s. According to legend the Count was born a prince of the house of Rákóczi in Transylvania, but the myths are murky. However, there has always been a profound fascination with the man supposed to have lived many lives under as many names, a man who appeared from nowhere with no past and no title and yet dazzled all of Europe. He appears here and there across the continent, then vanishes leaving behind whispers and lavish rumors touting his intellect, teachings, and hermetic expertise. It was said he was immortal, in possession of the Emerald Tablets, a Rosicrucian adept and alchemist, a spy, and a king in disguise. The Count was reluctant to discuss his past and his name but few were pressed to investigate this mysterious, charming, scholarly courtier as the Count's talents proved to be abundant and expert. Of the nobleman's past lives, St. John the Beloved apostle, Christian

Rosenkreuz (founder of the Rosicrucian Order), and Sir Francis Bacon are claimed to be among them.

    If an historical attempt is to be made of Count St.-Germain, it could be said that as a child he was sent to Italy, placed under the protection of Gian Gastone de Medici, the Grand Duke of Tuscany. It is speculated his life was in danger for his father had been forced into exile unable to defend his kingdom against the expansions of the Habsburg's empire. In Italy the Count received an exceptional education, attended the University of Siena, and became a virtuoso musician. He seemed to be fabulously wealthy; the Count appeared all over Europe and was present at the most unusual of occurrences. He would then disappear and resurface years later complete with new monikers and tales and feats of expert craftsmanship in a myriad of disciplines. There are even accounts of Count St.-Germain as having been in Egypt during Napoleon's campaign; supposedly the two were associated and the general kept a dossier on the Count. There exists a claim the ubiquitous yet elusive Count was in the American colonies, known as the Professor, and helped create the American flag! And this man whose origin was never revealed, whose past was non-existent, managed to disappear—simply evaporate—in 1784 without a trace.

NATURE: Chasing the Dream
ELEMENT: Air of Water
TETRAGRAMMATON: Vav
CARD PERSONAGE:
This card represents a young man or woman with light brown or dark blonde hair of varying shades, fair to medium complexion, and hazel eyes.

Keywords

Gallantry, strong sense of propriety, victory in romantic conquest. Highly creative and imaginative. Always searching and seeking. Positive messages from home or a loved one.

    If the Initiate of Cups represents a person: A companion, sibling, or good friend who is generous and dependable. A charming lover, a spiritual seeker. A hero or knight-in-shining-armor

The Adept of Cups

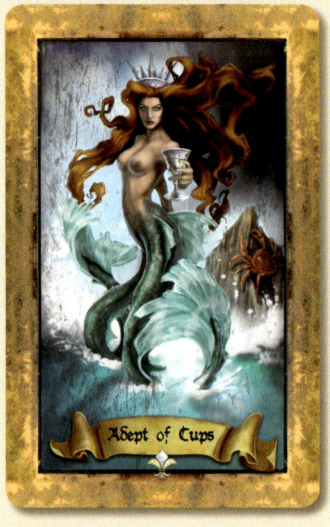

"Early in the ninth hour, fearlessly kiss my mouth and my cheeks, then I shall be redeemed, and be with you, my beloved bridegroom!"

—German Melusine Legend

Novelist Philippa Gregory wrote, "She is Melusina, the water goddess, and she is found in hidden springs and waterfalls in any forest in Christendom, even in those as far away as Greece." However, distinct legends of Melusina seem to evolve from areas forming medieval Germany, Britain, and France, three countries with close ties to the Frankish Merovingian dynasty from which it is said Melusina is descended. The different locations claim Melusine legends indigenous to the distinct locale, yet there are similar threads woven into these tapestries of folklore. French myth links Melusina with the Houses of Anjou, Lusignan, and Luxembourg. British Melusina intertwines within Arthurian tradition and the Plantagenet dynasty. Germanic mythology places Melusina atop Stollenburg Mountain near the castle of legendary Teutonic knight Peter von Staufenberg. German cleric Martin Luther believed another version of Melusina whom he referred to as a succubus. In all legends, Melusina marries. French tales maintain she married Angevin Fulk the Black, Guy de Lusignan, or Count Siegfried of the Ardennes. British lore tells of King Elynas, ruler of Scotland during the time of the crusades, and his marriage to Melusina's mother, the fair Pressyne. This take on the legend would indicate Melusina's father was a Scottish royal. And still yet, German fables tell of a wedding between the cavalier Peter von Staufenberg and Melusina. In all accounts, including the marriage of Melusina's mother to the Scottish king, the men are smitten and propose marriage. Melusina (as well as her mother) promise undying blissful love, but these nuptials reveal strict conditions for there is often a hard and fatal consequence committed to any coupling of a precious mystical being and a mere mortal. Once a month, on the Sabbath (Saturday), the men must not enter Melusina's or Pressyne's chambers for that is when the women bathed. In all the story variations, the spouses violate this taboo. This causes Melusina or her mother to flee, never to be seen by their partners again for their husbands have seen the fay women in their true state: fish or serpent from the waist down! Melusine disappears into the nearest body of water; Pressyne flees with her triplet daughters to the land of King Arthur—the lost Isle of Avalon.

NATURE: Motherly, nurturing
ELEMENT: Water of Water
TETRAGRAMMATON: Heh
CARD PERSONAGE:
This card is a general representation of a mature woman with hazel/blue eyes, blonde to light brown hair, fair to medium complexion, and of medium stature.

keywords

An emotionally secure situation. Safety, trust, and protection. Pleasure, happiness, success. Wise choices especially in relationships. All is out in the open, nothing is hidden.

If the Adept of Cups represents a person: A loving, protective matriarch, a devoted wife. A dependable, sensitive male friend. Trustworthy female companion, a woman involved in artistry.

The Mage of Cups

"According to Fredegar, Merovech was conceived when Choldio's wife went swimming and encountered a Quinotaur."

—*The Merovingian Kingdoms 450–751* by Ian Wood

Legend tells tale of a queen; some say her name was Argotta. One sun drenched day, this wife of Chlodio, king of the Salian Franks, was savaged while bathing in the seas by a Quinotaur, a mythical sea creature mentioned in the seventh century Frankish Chronicle of Fredegar, an anonymously authored manuscript that covers the history of the Merovingian dynasty. By brutalizing the wife of the Frankish king, the Beast of Neptune, a half-bull half-fish monster, was said to have fathered Merovech consequently siring the line of Merovingian kings.

The name "quinotaur" translates from Latin as "bull with five horns," which have been interpreted as representing the trident of Neptune: three horns flanked by the horns of the mythical bull, the Minotaur. Yet the legend of the Quinotaur can also be connected to the sea god Poseidon. A Phoenician legend recounts the disappearance of Europa, the granddaughter of Poseidon, and how she befriended a beautiful white bull that had mysteriously appeared on the beach. While riding the animal, Europa was carried off far into the sea to Crete where she gave birth to three sons fathered by the white bull. One of her sons, Minos, is recalled in Germanic mythology as having three sons of his own who became the ancestors of the Germanic people.

Many ancient historians claim the story of Europa was based on actual events and that she did indeed exist. Though this seems ridiculous to modern intellect, it is no less bizarre that the continent of Europe should have taken its name from this myth. One must take into account the story of Europa in conjunction with the story of the Quinotaur. The legend that begins with the abduction of Europa is completed by the myth of the Quinotaur who sires a race of sacred Frankish kings. For the Greeks, the sea bull of the Europa saga is seen as Zeus, the god traditionally personified as a bull as were many of the gods and kings of Phoenicia and Sumeria. Kings of ancient cultures in time became gods. Subsequently, the gods of prevailing cultures become the gods of less dominant societies. The sea bull of Europa is the Quinotaur of the Merovingian kings. As the Quinotaur was the legendary father of succeeding European monarchs, their mother was Europa after whom the sovereign dynasties named their continent.

NATURE: Fatherly
ELEMENT: Fire of Water
TETRAGRAMMATON: Yod
CARD PERSONAGE:
A mature or married man of physical and emotional stature, sporting varying shades of dark blonde, brown, to auburn hair, blue, or hazel eyes and a medium complexion.

keywords

Consideration, trustworthiness, and responsibility. A patriarchal dynamic, paternal instincts, dependability. Spiritual instruction. Security, calmness, protection, good advice.

If the Mage of Cups represents a person: A benevolent father, grandfather, or uncle. An honorable, dependable older male friend. An instructor, clergyman, sailor, artist, or designer.

The Pips

(Based on the Rosicrucian alchemy of Eudes Picard and Manly P. Hall)

Ace of Cups

Love blooms. Compassion is found. Healing begins. Joy is found where none existed. Fulfillment. Family, beauty. Discovering one's own destiny. Connecting to the artist within.

Two of Cups

Attraction, romance, proposals of marriage. Opposing forces come together. Union, cooperation, connection, partnership. Bonding friendships. Harmony, kindness to another.

Three of Cups

Support, reliance, dependability. Alliances, compromise, strong friendships. Happy conclusions, celebration. Achievement and success. Abundance, merriment, good times.

Four of Cups

Living in the past. Weariness, annoyance, boredom. Missed opportunities. Unfocused, distracted. Sluggishness, stagnation. Discontent, hesitancy. Refusal to make decisions.

Five of Cups

Breakthroughs, new possibilities. Assistance, gratitude, refreshment. Inheritance, new gain. Legacies, will, gifts. Don't worry over what cannot be changed. Fill the emptiness.

Six of Cups

Nurturing friendships, loving memories, nostalgia. Stroll down memory lane. Childhood, first loves, past influences. Courtship, new friends. Time to be light-hearted, time to be childlike.

Seven of Cups

Choices, multiple options. Learning to trust one's intuition and start prioritizing. Imagination, daydreams, unrealistic expectations. Wishful thinking, illusions of success.

Eight of Cups

Creative therapy, cleansing, recuperation. Modesty, shyness, timidity. Realization that now must be the time to discontinue effort, to walk away from the matter at hand. Time to rest.

Nine of Cups

Experience and confidence pay off! Abundance, earned achievement, enjoying the results of the fruits of labor. Fulfillment, happiness. Victory. Good health, loving family, success.

Ten of Cups

Connections, bonds, origins, homeland. Being aware of one's beginnings. Peace, love, family, and health mean more than material wealth. Honor and esteem. Reputation, contentment.

COINS
The Martinists

Differing from most mystery schools and hermetic fraternities, Martinism is explicitly focused on esoteric Christianity. It is an initiatic order based on Judeo-Christian mysticism and Cabala, and its teachings include the hermetic sciences, such as numerology, astrology, and the esoteric disciplines of Tarot, theurgy, and dream interpretation. The name of the order is derived from the French mystic and author Louis-Claude de Saint-Martin (1743–1803), who wrote under the pseudonym "The Unknown Philosopher." Martinist philosophy was formalized as an order during the late 1800s by Dr. Gérard Encausse and Augustin Chaboseau. Dr. Encausse later took on the mystical name "Papus" by which he is famously known.

Saint-Martin's writings are established on his individual experiences of the Divine going beyond the parameters of a church-defined theology and dogma. The philosopher discusses approaching God as a personal inner awakening to spirit-filled presence and he often refers to "*voie cardiaque*," the Way of the Heart. These writings parallel Gnostic teachings although there were no surviving Gnostic texts in Europe at that time. Saint-Martin's philosophical methodology offered unique insights into the nature of humankind, the cosmos, and the divine separately and within their interconnected relationship. One of the profound ideas conveyed in Martinist teachings is the principle of the Equilibrium of Opposites. Humankind entered the world of perceived duality of Divinity and Self when man partook of the proverbial forbidden fruit in the Garden of Eden, thus coming to know good and evil, light and darkness. Martinism delves into this duality deeply and fervently.

Dr. Gérard Encausse was born in Spain on July 13, 1865, to a Spanish mother and a French father, Louis Encausse, a chemist. His family moved to Paris when he was four years old, and he received his education there. As a young man, Encausse spent a great deal of time at the Bibliothèque Nationale in Paris studying the Kabbalah, occult tarot, magic, alchemy, and the writings of Eliphas Lévi. His circle of friends included Tsar Nicholas II and Tsarina Alexandra both as a physician and occult consultant plus a host of famous Parisian occultists.

The Novice of Coins

"Materialism has given us all that we can expect from it, and inquirers, disappointed as a rule, hope for great things from the future…"

—*The Tarot of the Bohemians*, Papus 1896

One of the most noteworthy hermeticians practicing during the historic occult movement of turn-of-the-century Paris was Dr. Gerard Encausse, known by his now famous nom de plume "Papus," a name taken from Eliphas Levi's work "Nuctemeron of Apollonius of Tyana" and theoretically translates as "physician." Encausse is primarily recognized as an author of books on magick, Cabala, and the Tarot, and as a prominent figure in the various occult organizations and Parisian spiritualist and literary circles that helped define the French capital in the late nineteenth century. Historically speaking, Papus' most noteworthy contribution to the world of secret societies and mystery schools was the founding of the modern Martinist Order.

Encausse was initiated into the discipline by Henri Delaage who was related by way of marriage and association to Louis-Claude de Saint-Martin, founder of the Martinist mystical initiation rites. Encausse, smitten with Saint-Martin's philosophy, created the magazine *L'Initiation*. The number of subscribers increased rapidly. Encausse then finished his medical education after which he completed his military service, and then went on to defend his medical dissertation. In 1891, Dr. Encausse formed an organization called *l'Ordre des Supérieurs Inconnus* of three degrees, generally known as the Order of Martinists, which was based on two extinct Masonic Rites: the Rite of Elect Coëns (Priests of Martinez de Pasqually) and the Rectified Rite of Saint-Martin. Saint-Martin was a student of Pasqually and wrote under the pseudonym "The Unknown Philosopher." Papus claimed to have come into the possession of the original papers of Pasqually and to have been given authority in the Rite of Saint-Martin by his friend Henri Delaage. Delaage claimed his maternal grandfather had been initiated into the order by Saint-Martin himself and had attempted to revive the order in 1887. The Martinist Order became Papus' dedicated raison d'être, his theurgic tradition, which continues to thrive.

The doctor never became a regular Freemason as he considered the fraternity to be atheistic. His belief in God was confirmed in 1893 when Papus was consecrated as a bishop of the Gnostic Church of France—an attempt to revive the Cathar religion of the ancient Languedoc.

NATURE: Learning, pupil, apprentice
ELEMENT: Earth of Earth
TETRAGRAMMATON: Heh
CARD PERSONAGE:
This card represents a young child or teenager of either sex,
dark complexioned and dark haired, sturdy build and deep eyes.

Keywords

Hungry for knowledge, eager for learning. Innate intelligence. New ideas, sound opinions and theories. Good news regarding health and/or finances. Planning for a career and the future.

If the Novice of Coins represents a person: A scholarly pupil or apprentice especially in the field of finance, botany, or animal husbandry. A messenger of good tidings. A child prodigy.

The Initiate of Coins

"All mystics speak the same language, for they come from the same country."

—Louis-Claude de Saint-Martin (1743–1803)

Born into a poor but noble family in Amboise, Louis-Claude de Saint-Martin came under the influence of Cabbalist Martinez de Pasqually while the former was stationed at a garrison in Bordeaux. Pasqually, an established mystic, founded a Masonic school based on the secrets of magical and theurgic rites. During September 1768, Saint-Martin was introduced to the Elect Coëns, a degree of highly initiated priests within the mystic order. From that year until 1771, Saint-Martin worked at Bordeaux as secretary to Martinez de Pasqually and eventually took charge of his Masonic fraternity when Pasqually left Bordeaux.

As a young man, in order to fulfill his father's wishes, Saint-Martin studied law but instead found a career as a lieutenant in the French army. It was while at a garrison in Bordeaux Saint-Martin met Pasqually and left the army in 1771 to become a teacher and philosopher of spirituality and mysticism.

He immersed himself in Masonic rites, travelled to England and Italy in his quest for knowledge, and circulated among the theosophical elite. His first book *Errors and Truth*, written under Saint-Martin's nom de plume "the Unknown Philosopher," was well received and hailed as a bible of Masonic science by occultists in France and Germany.

After much travel, Saint-Martin settled in Versailles in 1778. That year he published his second book in which he examined the correlations between man, nature, and divinity bringing to bear the purpose of the evolutionary scheme as a realization of man's god-like nature. In 1784, the Philalethians invited Saint-Martin as a member, however, he refused due to their interest in psychic phenomena; he felt the society lacked the ethics necessary to achieve spiritual perfection as he believed moral development to be the true basis of occultism. By 1790, Saint-Martin later eschewed all Masonry asking that his name be removed from the registers; Masonry did not agree with his profound spiritual philosophy. The thought around which the life of Saint-Martin revolved was compassion for the suffering of humanity, faith in its ultimate destiny and journey back to the spiritual source. Saint-Martin taught to look within in the search for God, for "man is the only true witness and positive sign by which the Supreme Universal Source may be known."

NATURE: Glory in labor
ELEMENT: Air of Earth
TETRAGRAMMATON: Vav
CARD PERSONAGE:
This card represents a young man, tanned, roughhewn or muscular, dark hair, and dark brown to black eyes.

Keywords

Time to work! Careful planning proves fruitful. Industriousness, productivity, ambition. Patience, responsibility, methodical. Trustworthy, thorough. News concerning inheritance.

If the Initiate of Coins represents a person: A handyman, carpenter, farmer, craftsman. Contractor, designer, mechanic, electrician. Automotive worker. A good providing husband.

The Adept of Coins

"The Sophia of the Way of the Heart is a feminine image of the Divine."

—Steven Armstrong, Martinist

Central to the teachings of the Martinist Order is a philosophy known as the Way of the Heart, what some scholars refer to as the Sophia Tradition. Sophia, or Wisdom, has many meanings. One of these is the Gnostic myth of Sophia in which she is an Aeon, emanated from and realized by the First Cause thus giving birth to the material world. As Wisdom, Sophia is also one of the four cardinal virtues; her name embodies the love of Wisdom. The Sophia of the Way of the Heart is the Divine Feminine. Her origins have been obscured by the winds of endless time, however, as the Divine Feminine, Sophia can be linked to virtually every era, culture, and society: Isis, Inanna, Hecate, Ishtar, Maat, Hera, Juno, Demeter, and Persephone.

Surprisingly, Sophia is a consistent theme in monotheism, threading her way through the mystical traditions of Judaism and Christianity. Both theologies consider Sophia the feminine manifestation of the divine. She appears throughout

Hebrew scripture. Students of Cabala will immediately recognize Wisdom as the second sephirot, Chokhmah, on the Tree of Life. In second century BC, Egyptian king Ptolemy II ordered the Hebrew Scriptures translated into Greek by the Jewish community of Alexandria. The work became known as the Septuagint. In this, Chokhmah was translated as Sophia. She appears in Proverbs: "Wisdom has built herself a home; she has carved her seven pillars. She has prepared her food, spiced her wine, and she has set her table." In Judaism, she is the Shekhinah, ruling from the Heavens and here on Earth. In Christianity, Sophia is often envisioned as the Virgin Mary. In Neoplatonism, Sophia is interpreted as the Holy Wisdom/Logos incarnate in the Christ. During the nineteenth century, a group of Russian mystical theologians endeavored to integrate Sophia as one of the aspects of the Holy Trinity. In fact, Christian Russia has historically venerated Sophia, dedicating to her a church in Kiev—The Cathedral of St. Sophia. Gnostics proclaim that as God came to Earth in human form as Jesus, so Sophia appeared as his partner and consort, Mary Magdalene. Also known as the Grail Goddess, Sophia's feast day is November 28. She is symbolized most often by a dove, crescent moon, stars, a cup, or tree.

NATURE: Fertility, home/hearth
ELEMENT: Water of Earth
TETRAGRAMMATON: Heh
CARD PERSONAGE:
This card represents a mature woman, olive skinned, rich chestnut to dark brown hair, and deep, dark eyes. She can be married or unmarried.

keywords

Robust fitness. Good diet. Fertility, children. Healthy pregnancy and birth. A well-kept and happy home. Confidence, sincerity, assuredness, boldness. Security, comfort, safety.

If the Adept of Coins represents a person: A happy home-maker. A successful professional mother-figure. A bank manager, stock broker, or accountant. A gardener, herbalist, or botanist.

The Mage of Coins

"The name of God is YHVH. If you wish to write about God, observe nature. The divine spirit is a power that cannot be expressed in human language."

—Jacob Boehme (1575–1624)

Martinism itself is a system of mystical Christian Illuminist philosophy and practice based upon the original foundational teachings of Jacob Boehme. Martinists, being members of an esoteric Christian fraternity, maintain a strong belief in God. However, they perceive the one God as being composed of a dualist nature: light/darkness, bliss/suffering, good/evil. Martinist philosophy believes the secondary dualist nature of the One gives birth to a third entity expressing its own eternal desire to be; this third entity mystically strives to be reunited with the One and seeks to restore man's relationship with the Creator. In Martinism this is accomplished through the elevation of spiritual consciousness through a structured system of initiatic rituals. These progressive initiations bring one to a state of enlightenment in which the initiate is spiritually receptive to divine experience. Accompanying these degrees of initiation, a wide range of hermetic sciences are taught and utilized including meditative prayer, symbolism, numerology, Cabala, alchemy, and astrology.

Concerning a First Cause or God, Martinism integrates the traditions of Christian theologians such as the Divine Trinity. However, Martinist philosophy is gnostic nature; the Trinity is regarded more as emanations. Martinist doctrine affirms the equal necessity of faith and knowledge and proposes divine grace, in order to be effective, must be enacted by the free intelligent will of the individual human being. Martinist doctrine rejects reincarnation as such, but its principles interpret the journey of the human soul as "reintegration." Reintegration is the belief that although mankind fell from grace, we are not abandoned by the Creator. God maintains a connection to all though an inherent desire for reconciliation profoundly imparted within the spiritual psyche. The Martinist reunion of man and the Divine can be achieved by transformation of the soul during a continuous spiritual progression. Through initiation, study, and personal reflection Martinism seeks to demonstrate the philosophy of Reintegration and transformation—the process of spiritual healing and becoming whole again with the Creator, to return to Godhead becoming one with the Divine.

NATURE: Benevolent Power
ELEMENT: Fire of Earth
TETRAGRAMMATON: Yod
CARD PERSONAGE:

This card represents an older man, most likely married, olive skinned, dark brown to black hair, and broad physical stature.

Keywords

Excellent financial skills, generosity, patience, loyalty. Wealth, possessions. Sound investment strategies. Financial assistance. Monetary opportunities present themselves.

If the Mage of Coins represents a person: Financial advisor, entrepreneur, banking executive, farming/ranching industrialist. A father or older family member coming to the aid of a relative.

The Pips

(Based on the Martinist philosophy of Papus)

Ace of Coins

Prosperous times begin. Contentment takes root. Sudden wealth, new enterprises that prove fruitful. New dwellings, attainment, accomplishment. Success is assured. Material gain.

Two of Coins

Difficulty balancing financial matters. Confusion in the home. Discord, anxiety, obstacles. Opposing forces try to reach an agreement. Absence of harmony, lack of cooperation. Insecurity.

Three of Coins

Generous actions, noble deeds, good character. Proficiency, pride in one's work, craftsmanship. Skill and mastery. Success through labor. Distinction, celebrity, recognition.

Four of Coins

Living in the past. Weariness, annoyance, boredom. Missed opportunities. Unfocused, distracted. Sluggishness, stagnation. Discontent, hesitancy. Refusal to make decisions.

five of Coins

Breakthroughs, new possibilities. Assistance, gratitude, refreshment. Inheritance, new gain. Legacies, will, gifts. Don't worry over what cannot be changed. Fill the emptiness.

Six of Coins

Spiritual healing. Completely in the moment. Immediate gratification. Living for today, all momentum in the present. Spontaneity, ons yet attentive, careful, vigilant.

Seven of Coins

Choices, multiple options. Learning to trust one's intuition and start prioritizing. Imagination, daydreams, unrealistic expectations. Wishful thinking, illusions of success.

Eight of Coins

Creative therapy, cleansing, recuperation. Modesty, shyness, timidity. Realization that now must be the time to discontinue effort, to walk away from the matter at hand. Time to rest.

Nine of Coins

Experience and confidence pay off! Abundance, earned achievement, enjoying the results of the fruits of labor. Fulfillment, happiness. Victory. Good health, loving family, success.

Ten of Coins

Connections, bonds, origins, homeland. Being aware of one's beginnings. Peace, love, family, and health mean more than material wealth. Honor and esteem. Reputation, contentment.

WANDS
The Golden Dawn

The roots of modern occult Tarot run deeply into the earth of France beginning with the occult revival of the 1700s through 1800s. Commencing with Court de Gébelin (the first alternative occult history of the Tarot) and his student, the father of Tarot divination, Etteilla, to the secret fraternities of nineteenth century Paris boasting noted occultists as Paul Christian, Eliphas Levi, Stanislas de Guaita, Oswald Wirth, and Papus, the Tarot began its journey across the Channel to Victorian England. This pivotal time in Tarot history had much to do with the voluminous occult writings of hermetician Eliphas Levi. These ample works were translated, "corrected," and adapted by three dedicated British occultists: A. E. Waite, William Wynn Westcott, and Aleister Crowley. These three men would later become integral to the inner workings of a fledgling Hermetic Order of the Golden Dawn.

The three founding fathers of the Golden Dawn were Freemason and Rosicrucians; they were William Robert Woodman, William Wynn Westcott, and Samuel MacGregor Mathers. The first temple, the Isis-Urania Temple, was founded in London in 1888. The Golden Dawn was one of few secret societies to allow women as participants in equality with men. This may be due to the story that permission to establish the order was given by prominent Rosicrucian and German countess, Anna Sprengel, to her English envoy and fellow occult enthusiast Wynn Westcott. Wait was initiated into the order in 1891, and Crowley joined him later in 1898. The order was established upon the founders' versions of the teachings of Levi and Egyptian mystery schools. These philosophies were articulated in the order's foundational documents, the Cipher Manuscripts, describing outlines for grade rituals and the hermetic sciences such as Cabala, astrology, occult and divinatory Tarot, geomancy, and alchemy.

The Golden Dawn flourished at the turn of the century, however, by 1900 many members were dissatisfied by Mather's leadership and close friendship with the disorderly Crowley; the Golden Dawn began to disintegrate. Remaining loyalists helped to reinvent the order in London and due to their efforts, the Golden Dawn continues to thrive to this day in its many guises and orders.

The Novice of Wands

> "Some of our Lady Members are the most advanced. One of Jewish extraction is, I think, the most advanced of all."
>
> —Reverend William Ayton, Member Golden Dawn (1888)

Moina Mathers was born Mina Bergson on February 28, 1865, to Polish Jew Michel Gabriel Bergson and Irish-Jewish Katherine Levison in Geneva, Switzerland. She was the fourth of seven children born to the distinguished musical genius and his wife. Moina's brother, Henri, went on to become a brilliant philosopher, lecturer, and writer and had earned for himself a position within the faculty of the prestigious College of France. Another brother had become a medical doctor in Berlin, and yet another an accomplished actor in the United States.

Like her father and brothers, Moina also exhibited extraordinary talents that manifested at a young age, demonstrated through her artwork. Following her artistic path, she went on to graduate from the esteemed Slade School of Art of London University. Moina developed a passion for Egyptian art and antiquities and would leave her apartment in the West End to immerse herself in London's museums, galleries, and reading rooms that fed her hunger for all things Egyptian. This desire ultimately led to a chance meeting of remarkable proportions, historic in the world of occult sciences and philosophies. In 1887, while studying at the British Museum, she chanced to encounter a frequent patron, a gentleman by the name of Samuel Liddell "MacGregor" Mathers. A year later, Mathers founded the Hermetic Order of the Golden Dawn, one of the most influential organizations espousing the Western Mystery Tradition. In March 1888, the order inducted its first initiate—Moina. Her chosen motto was "*Vestigia Nulla Retrorsum,*" meaning "Prudence never retraces its steps." A year later, in 1890, she married S. L. Mathers and Mina Bergson became Moina Mathers. Moina, as a clairvoyant, often divined her husband's visions and spiritual evocations and artistically interpreted them as an illustrator. In 1918, when Mathers died, most likely from a case of influenza, Moina took over the Alpha et Omega, a successor organization to the Golden Dawn, as its Imperatrix. She died in 1928 in London. Moina enjoyed a life-long friendship with Annie Elizabeth Fredericka Horniman, a well-known patron of the London theatre, significant member of the Hermetic Order of the Golden Dawn until her resignation in 1903, and good friend and secretary to W. B. Yeats.

NATURE: Opportunistic beginnings, brilliance
ELEMENT: Earth of Fire
TETRAGRAMMATON: Heh
CARD PERSONAGE:
This card represents a child, adolescent or teenager, fair haired and skinned, with hazel or blue eyes.

Keywords

Vibrant enthusiasm, energetic talent. Passion, optimism. Zealous, daring, resourceful, enterprising. Positive news from afar, usually concerning business or current enterprise.

If the Novice of Wands represents a person: Likely a first born, highly gifted child with great potential. A prodigy. A public or motivational speaker. A young, idealistic philosopher. A fervent student.

The Initiate of Wands

"As far as I was concerned, Mathers was my only link with the Secret Chiefs to whom I was pledged."

—From the diary of Aleister Crowley

London was ripe, ready to follow in the footsteps of the Parisian occult revival. Samuel Liddell "MacGregor" Mathers, one of the original founders of the Hermetic Order of the Golden Dawn, was born in 1854 in London, England. Later in life, Mathers added the "MacGregor" surname to announce his Highland Scottish heritage, although there is little evidence of this in his family background. As a young adult, he had a keen interest in military strategies and theories of war, his first manuscript being a translation of a French military manual. In 1877, Mathers was initiated into Freemasonry at Bournemouth in the Lodge of Hengest No. 195. Mathers progressed to Master Mason fairly quickly but for reasons unknown, Mathers resigned from the lodge in 1882. Shortly after, he was introduced to doctors Wynn Westcott and William Woodman, both high-ranking Masons, who introduced Mathers to the Societas Rosicruciana, an exclusive organization open to Master Masons. Here Mathers met Fredrick Hockley, a proficient crystal gazer. Mathers would later perfect his own art of scrying: divining in the spirit realm with the use of a specific translucent device. Mathers was a gifted polyglot. With the help of Westcott, Mathers translated Von Rosenroth's Kabbalah Denudata. At this time Mathers formed his pathway to the Secret Chiefs of the Third Order, supernatural adepts who oversaw the magickal work of the Golden Dawn. It was Westcott, Mathers, and Woodman who formed the governing body of the original Hermetic Order of the Golden Dawn; this was a prolific time for Mathers. He completed his first significant literary work—*The Kaballa Denudata;* he helped create the Golden Dawn, and he met his future wife, Mina Bergson, for the first time at the British Museum. She, from an intellectually prominent Swiss/French family, was at the British Museum studying Egyptian art. After a short engagement, the two were married after which Mina then adopted the Anglican name of "Moina." Moina was an important life-long partner of Mathers and she was one of the most influential and knowledgeable members of the Golden Dawn, well versed in its philosophy. After her husband's death years later, Moina Mathers moved back to Paris and kept the core tenets and practices of the true order flourishing through other fraternal commitments.

NATURE: Bravado, Adventure
ELEMENT: Air of Fire
TETRAGRAMMATON: Vav
CARD PERSONAGE:
This card represents a young strapping man or woman, light complexioned with blonde to red hair, brown to blue eyes.

Keywords

Impulsive, spontaneous. Seeking, exploring, extended journeys—either geographically, physically, or spiritually. Change of jobs, domiciles, or romantic partners. Daring, dynamic.

If the Initiate of Wands represents a person: A member of the military, entertainment, or travel industry. A commercial pilot or flight attendant, cruise ship employee. An ambitious intern.

The Adept of Wands

"I, Isis, am all that hath been, that is or shall be. I, who made light from my feathers, the wind from my wings, no mortal man ever hath me unveiled!—until now."

—Inscription–Isis Temple at Sais, Egypt

Isis—the Goddess of the Throne. Her name in its original Egyptian etymology meant "throne" and was personified by her headdress, which was later replaced by a Sun disc centered between two horns. The myth and lore of the Egyptian goddess-queen, Isis, simmers at the very core of Golden Dawn philosophy. Deeply immersed in the honor of "Isis Magick," order initiates are devout in their veneration of this most ancient and magnificent of female deities. Introduced to Rome in 86 BCE, Isis-worship has endured the whirling sands of time and passage of millennia. For almost 3,500 years the wife and sister of Osiris, the mother of Horus, ruled as the goddess-queen of Egypt presiding over its ruling dynasties and kingdoms.

The goddess Isis has become metaphor for all things magickal, feminine, and fertile. She personifies the faithful wife and devoted mother. She is Mistress of the Mystical Realm and the Spirit of Nature. She brought hope to slaves, sinners, and those oppressed. She was worshipped by the aristocracy and royalty, artisans and magicians. Isis is also known as protector of the dead and goddess of children. As the embodiment of the throne, Isis was a symbol representative of ruling pharaohs and their governance. The kings were the children of Isis and sat on her throne.

The goddess Isis was born on the Fourth Day, the first daughter of Geb (god of the Earth) and Nut (goddess of the Sky). She married her brother, Osiris, and together they had a son, Horus. When Osiris was murdered by Set, Isis gathered his strewn body parts and, utilizing her magical powers, restored his body to life thus resurrecting him.

The adoration of Isis eventually spread throughout the Greco-Roman world, until the suppression of paganism during the spread of Christianity. One of the theories regarding the Black Madonnas of medieval Europe is that these depictions of Madonna and child are actually cloaked icons built or painted in honor of Isis and Horus, continuing the veneration of the Egyptian goddess under the ever-watchful eyes of an oppressive church. The same could be said for the myriad depictions of Madonna and child chiseled and painted throughout antiquity. The Magdalene has also been associated with Isis as a goddess, wife of a king and mother to future kings.

NATURE: Inner Grace, Outer Beauty
ELEMENT: Water of Fire
TETRAGRAMMATON: Heh
CARD PERSONAGE:
This card represents a mature, handsome woman, as likely to be single as she is married, possessed of blue or grey eyes and reddish blonde hair.

Keywords

Graciousness, independence, self-confidence. Mentally and physically dynamic. Quiet dignity, the power of attraction, spiritual creativity, personal magnetism. Compassion, warmth.

If the Adept of Wands represents a person: A strong, protective, motivational mother-figure. Businesswoman; planning, production, or performing within the arts, humanities, and sciences.

The Mage of Wands

> "It is beyond dispute that Osiris made his worshipers dream strange things of him, and that he possessed their bodies and souls forever."
>
> —Frank Belknap Long
> from *The Mummy Walks Among Us,* 1971, by Vic Ghidalia

Equally important to the magickal system of the Golden Dawn is the husband and brother of Isis, the Egyptian deity-king Osiris. Osiris was one of four children begotten by the earth god Geb and Nut, the goddess of the sky and heavens: Osiris, Isis, Set, and Nepthys. Osiris is usually identified as the god of the afterlife, the underworld, and the dead. Osiris was at times considered the eldest son of the sun-god Ra and the sky goddess Nut, as well as being brother and husband of Isis, and Horus being his posthumously begotten son.

Osiris was the eldest son and so became king of Egypt, taking his sister Isis as his bride and queen. As legend tells it, Osiris' brother Set was terribly jealous of his brother, the king. Set cast a spell, transforming himself into a hellish beast and attacked his brother, ripping him to shreds and casting his body parts throughout Egypt. Set then proclaimed himself to be god-king of Egypt, taking his sister Nepthys as his wife. However, Set underestimated the bond between his two sisters and the great magickal powers of Isis. Together, the two sisters roamed the country, collecting the battered fragments of Osiris' body. Working her magickal powers, Isis reassembled her husband's body and breathed life back into her brother. He was resurrected and Isis soon became pregnant with Horus. In this regard, she was at that point considered to be a virgin and the delivery a virgin birth, the impregnation accomplished by Osiris' spirit. There are "coincidences" regarding this birth: Horus and Jesus (similar names) were both said to be born on December 25, or the winter solstice, and born of a virgin. The similarities continue: both were the "only begotten son" of a god (Osiris and Yahweh), both had their coming announced to their mothers by an angel—Horus' birth was heralded by the star Sirius (the morning star) and Jesus' birth was foreshadowed by a star in the east (the sun rises in the east), Horus was visited at birth by "three solar deities" and Jesus was visited by "three wise men," and as infants both Horus and Jesus were marked for assassination, Horus by Herut and Jesus by Herod. There are many more parallels, too many to be discussed here, and enough to cause one to pause and think . . . could the life of Jesus be based on the royal Egyptian family of Osiris, Isis, and Horus?

NATURE: Industrious, Dynamic
ELEMENT: Fire of Fire
TETRAGRAMMATON: Yod
CARD PERSONAGE:
This card represents a mature man, very likely married; the outdoors type with blue, or hazel eyes and reddish to strawberry blonde hair.

Keywords

Business savvy, leadership qualities, executive talents. Financial aid. Excellent foundations for enterprise. Socially active. Generosity, nobility. Possible inheritance.

If the Mage of Wands represents a person: Advertising executive, inventor, marketing or sales director, idea person, concept development, entrepreneur. A firm authoritarian, yet fair and kind.

The Pips

(Based on the magickal interpretations of the Tarot de Marseille by Golden Dawn initiates S. L. MacGregor Mathers and Israel Regardie)

Ace of Wands

Root of the powers of fire. Projects take root. Plans begin to flourish. Circumstances are right for enterprise. Inheritance of money or property. Strength, vigor, and energy. Natural force.

Two of Wands

Influence, dominion over others. Boldness, determination, grit. Turbulence, restlessness, fierceness. Revenge, unyielding, immovable. Obstacles, opposition, resistance. Polarity, schism.

Three of Wands

The foundation of strength. Arrogance, pride, and control. Strong self-realization, establishment of power. Maturity and wisdom is the key to successful negotiations.

Four of Wands

Achievement, perfected work. Toil and labor complete—rest now possible. Success in settlements. Conclusions drawn from knowledge. Ideas once manifested now end in completion.

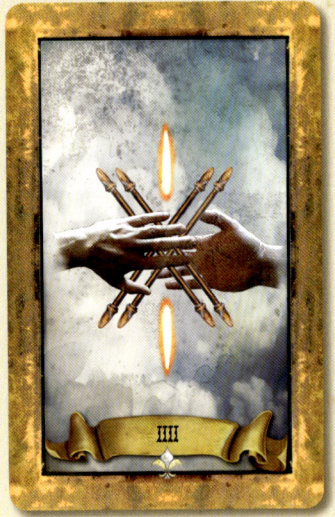

Five of Wands

Strife, quarrels, arguments. Infighting, back-stabbing, ill-willed rivalry. Rashness, cruelty, violence. Competition for financial gain, struggle for wealth and fortune. Immature decisions.

Six of Wands

Victory, hope fulfilled. A solid win. Affairs manipulated to successful end. Triumph after labor and effort. Rewards and recognition received. Pride in one's accomplishments. Sociability.

Seven of Wands

Valor, courage, bravery when confronting existing opposition. Overcoming obstacles, meeting problems head-on. Confidence when outnumbered. Present upheavals dealt with.

Eight of Wands

Swiftness, hastiness. Too much force applied rapidly. Impulsive decisions. Time to take action before events move too quickly. Make haste. Arousal, keen awareness. Passage of time.

Nine of Wands

Great strength and rejuvenation. Robust health, recovery from illness. Tremendous, unshakable power—possible inflexibility. Physical attractiveness, pride in one's appearance.

Ten of Wands

Oppression, subjugation. Cruelty, spite towards another, injustice. Selfish gain. Manipulation. Failure when confronting opposition. Lying, slander, jealousy, malice.

The roots of the Freemasonic Fraternity is a hotly debated topic, where lively debate exists primarily between two camps: those who adhere to the fables of Hiram Abiff, the builder of Solomon's Temple, and the school of thought espousing the legendary exploits of the Templars. The concept regarding the Knights as being precursors to Freemasonry is backed by many volumes of well researched and valid theory. Basically speculated, the harbored Templar fleet laden with treasure disappeared from La Rochelle, France, in 1307, after the order was arrested by papal decree issued in collusion with King Philip IV. A portion of the escaping fleet, with its crew of Templars, found its way to the fiords of Scotland where, it is said, the warrior monks aided Robert the Bruce, King of Scotland, in his inexplicable victory over the massive forces of England's Edward II. The Templar alignment with the royal house of Scotland would seem logical as both were excommunicated from the church. It was 1314, the Battle of Bannockburn, and Scotland's minute cavalry and infantry were no match for the English sovereign's military might. However, the English forces were not expecting a surprise attack by a well mounted Templar cavalry and the Scots were led to an unbelievable victory still celebrated to this day.

The Templars eventually came under the control of the St. Clair (Sinclair) noble family of Rosslyn, Scotland. Legend holds they voyaged together and were the first to set foot on the upper eastern coast of North America, one hundred years before Columbus' voyage. There has been evidence discovered in areas such as Nova Scotia, Montreal, Minnesota, Massachusetts, and New Hampshire that attests to Templar/Sinclair exploration and possible settlement.

It is said Scotland is the birthplace of Freemasonry. The Templars were superbly skilled architects and builders; it is highly possible non-seafaring Templars left in Scotland went "underground" for their own safety, then went on to emerge in interconnected lodges of Scottish Freemasonry where their knowledge of sacred geometry could be practiced in secret and their vast hordes of treasure guarded and protected. In fact, the oldest established Masonic lodge in the world was built in 1500s' Edinburgh, Scotland…in the heart of Templar country.

The Novice of Swords

"The secrets can only be revealed in the presence of three: King Solomon, Hiram the King of Tyre, and myself."

—Hiram Abiff, Architect, Solomon's Templ

Masonic "Blue Lodges" offer the pledge three degrees of initiation: the Entered Apprentice, Fellowcraft, and Master Mason Degrees. The third degree, the Master Mason, is based on the fabled master Mason Hiram Abiff. Although there is no mention of Abiff in scripture, the Masonic account is said to be based upon the Bible. According to legend, Hiram Abiff arrived in Jerusalem and was appointed chief architect by King Solomon, overseeing the construction of the king's temple. Legend tells of three fellowcraft masons who lied in wait for Abiff. They ambushed him, demanding the secrets of a master mason and the keys to sacred geometry. During the struggle, Abiff refused to disclose his mysteries. His attackers each hit the architect with a mason's tool. He was incapacitated by the first two assailants and struck dead by the last. The assailants hid Abiff's corpse beneath a mound of debris then returned later to move the body and bury it in a shallow grave marked with a branch of acacia. At the Temple site, the master's presence was missed the following morning, which prompted King Solomon to expedite a search party of fellowcraft masons to hunt for the missing architect. The burial location was accidentally discovered, and Abiff's cadaver was exhumed to be given a decent interment. The three assailants were caught shortly after by another search party as they tried to make their escape by fleeing on the road to Joppa. They were captured and brought to justice. Solomon informed his work force the secrets of the Master Mason were lost and he replaced them with substitutes based on gestures given and words exchanged upon the discovery of Abiff's body.

At the end of the third degree Masonic ritual, the Lodge Master approaches the candidate and stands very close to him, pressing his right breast and foot against the candidate's. Placing his left hand on the initiate's back, The Lodge Master then recites the Five Points of Fellowship: "Hand to hand I greet you as a brother; foot to foot I will support you in all your undertakings; knee to knee, the posture of my daily supplications shall remind me of your wants; breast to breast, your lawful secrets when entrusted to me as such I will keep as my own; and hand over back, I will support your character in your absence as in your presence."

NATURE: Diplomacy, solutions
ELEMENT: Earth of Air
TETRAGRAMMATON: Heh
CARD PERSONAGE:
This card represents a wide-eyed, tall child, adolescent, or teenager, medium complexioned, with varying shades of brown hair and eyes.

keywords

News of a solution! Concern for others, discernment, diplomacy, understanding. Problematic matters resolved, crisis management. Imaginative, creative, objective. Good health.

If the Novice of Swords represents a person: Lawyer, probation or police officer, envoy, diplomat, investigator. Trouble-shooter or repair person. Computer programmer, architect.

The Initiate of Swords

"The Regulars are coming out!"

—Paul Revere, April 1775, the midnight ride from Lexington to Concord, Massachusetts, in the American Colonies

American patriot Paul Revere never finished the infamous ride that has come to be synonymous with the dawn of the American Revolution. Paul Revere was galloping his mare to Lexington to warn of a British invasion, knocking at each house and greeting inhabitants with the whisper "The Regulars are coming out!" the "Regulars" being the encroaching British troops. In Lexington, Revere was joined by two other nationalists, William Dawes and Dr. Samuel Prescott. They accompanied Revere on his mission to Concord when the trio was intercepted by a British patrol. Dawes managed to escape almost immediately, Prescott soon after; Revere didn't escape until much later sans his mare. He walked back to Lexington, arriving in time to witness part of the battle on Lexington Green. Dawes lost his way in the misty blackness of the New England night and his destination eluded him. Dr. Samuel Prescott was the only messenger out of the trio who reached Concord where his warning was delivered.

Not widely known about the Revolutionary hero Paul Revere, he was one of the first York Rite Freemasons in colonial Massachusetts when he became a Royal Arch Mason and Knight Templar on December 11, 1769. This is according to the records of St. Andrew's Royal Arch Chapter, Boston, Massachusetts. He also served as Most Worshipful Grand Master of The Grand Lodge of Massachusetts from December 12, 1794, to December 27, 1797. According to today's Central Intelligence Agency, Paul Revere founded the first patriot intelligence network on record, a Boston-based group known as the "mechanics." Prior to the American Revolution, Revere had been a member of the Sons of Liberty, a political organization that actively opposed incendiary tax legislation, such as the Stamp Act of 1765. Beginning in 1774, the "mechanics" spied on British soldiers and met regularly in the legendary Green Dragon Tavern, which had been purchased by the St. Andrew's Lodge in 1764. The Masonic Square and Compass adorned the front door as well as a copper dragon that had turned green with weathering. With its pub downstairs and the lodge occupying the upper floor, historians have christened the ale house "the headquarters of the American Revolution."

NATURE: Courageous, Warrior
ELEMENT: Air of Air
TETRAGRAMMATON: Vav
CARD PERSONAGE:
This card represents a young man or woman, medium complexioned with varying shades of brown hair, brown or hazel eyes.

Keywords

Solutions. Intellectual and mental finesse. Genius, brilliance, superiority. Overcoming complications. A warning of opposition or hostility. Bravado, heroic actions, valor, courage.

If the Initiate of Swords represents a person: The Equalizer, the Enforcer. Member of the armed forces or police/sheriffs'/state troopers' department. Administrator, manager, analyst.

The Adept of Swords

"I would hope to glorify freedom and liberty over there [America] in the hope that it may be regained over here [France]."

—Frederic-Auguste Bartholdi
Artist and creator of the Statue of Liberty

She towers ever vigilant above the waves. Dauntless, tall, and strong—facing all of humanity with clear, cold, serene eyes. The winds carry her silent call to the four corners of the world: give me your tired, your poor, your huddled masses yearning to breathe free. The Colossus of New York Harbor, Lady Liberty, clutches her tablet close to her and holds aloft the Torch of Light so those with eyes to see may read the wisdom of the ages. However, without Swords' lending its properties of intellect to support wisdom, the Protectress' beacon would be useless. An early "Lady Liberty" was depicted in 1861 by Currier and Ives, titled *The Spirit of '61—God, Our Country and Liberty* and she is indeed brandishing a sword in her right hand instead of a torch.

The Statue of Liberty is a gift that was bestowed by the French, a massive, definitive declaration that the Masonic experiment was truly a success. The seeds of freedom—both religious and personal—and the pursuit of life, liberty, and happiness (the ideals of European and British Rosicrucians, Freemasons, and mystics) had been planted in the soil of the newly founded New Jerusalem, the United States of America, and had blossomed to fruition. This was the goal of her founding fathers, many of whom were Freemasons themselves. Sculptor and Freemason Frederic-Auguste Bartholdi was engaged by fellow Mason Edouard de Laboulaye to take on the immense task of creating this magnificent endowment which paid homage not only to the American philosophy and way of life, but also the Roman goddess, Libertas. The massive statuary itself, made of iron and coated with a layer of copper, follows classic Greek and Roman design.

In 1865, Edouard de Laboulaye (a French political scholar and US *Constitution* expert) proposed a monument be built as an accolade from France to the United States to commemorate its perseverance of freedom and democracy. Together, Bartholdi and Laboulaye hoped that by recognizing the recent accomplishments of the United States, the French would be moved to find the inspiration and courage to create their own democracy in the face of a deeply entrenched dictatorial monarchy. It was the hope of many French liberals that democracy would triumph—freedom and justice for all would become their inalienable birthright.

NATURE: Reserved, Tranquil
ELEMENT: Water of Air
TETRAGRAMMATON: Heh
CARD PERSONAGE:
This card represents a tall, graceful, beautiful woman, likely to be divorced, possessed of brown eyes and brown to sandy or dark blonde hair.

Keywords

Sincere communication. Perceptive, observant, vigilant, determined, decisive, honest. Strong-willed, focused, quick witted, efficient. Intellect, integrity. Independence, liberation.

If the Adept of Swords represents a person: Mature woman in a position of power and authority. Single mother, step-mother, widow. Musician, surgeon, nurse, or teacher. Editor, negotiator.

The Mage of Swords

"He who wears the lambskin as a badge of a Mason is thereby continually reminded of purity of life and conduct which is essentially necessary to his gaining admission into that celestial Lodge above, where the Supreme Architect of the universe presides."

—Malcom C. Duncan, Masonic Ritual and Monitor

There exist parallels between Freemasonry and Martinism as one is the forerunner of the other, acting as an initiatic paradigm upon which its descendant fraternity is modeled. There are significant differences between the two, especially regarding theological philosophies, but the primary variance that directly influences each of the orders' degree systems is their concepts and principles concerning "God."

The Martinist Order is a mystical Christian fraternity firm in its belief in the triune God and that Deity, at times, takes on a distinct male persona—God being referred to as the Father and Jesus as the Son. The fraternities of Freemasonry do not make that distinction; the theosophical tenets of Freemasonry specifically ask that the order's members recognize a higher power as each initiate interprets that Divine Will. In order to qualify this philosophy of an ineffable Power and in accordance with the basic foundations of Freemasonry, God is referred to as "The Grand (or Great) Architect of the Universe." In that respect, TGAOTU can be male, female, both, or gender neutral. It is surprising, however, that an exclusively all-male fraternity does indeed place a good deal of emphasis on the divine feminine perspective and Freemasonry is rich in its sacred symbolism. The Statue of Liberty is a prime example of this. The city of Washington, DC, is known for being laid out and constructed according to Masonic architectural sacred geometry. This metropolis is rife with statues and monuments depicting classic Greek and Roman variations of goddesses. In fact, this capital city of the great Masonic effort—the United States of America—was named for the "goddess" Columbia (District of Columbia). Actually, "Columbia" is the historical and poetic name used for the United States of America and also one of the names of its female personification. Taking this a step further, if the founding Freemasons of the United States knew of early explorations of the Knights Templar on the North American continent, then they surely would have been aware of the Knights' suggested knowledge of an occult star, a magical star, which the warrior monks learned about from manuscripts plundered from beneath the temple mount. The name of this star—La Merica.

NATURE: Power, Position
ELEMENT: Fire of Air
TETRAGRAMMATON: Yod
CARD PERSONAGE:
This card represents a mature professional man of status with dark hair and eyes.

keywords

In command, take control, communicate. Scruples, intellect, ethics, decisiveness. Logical, analytical. Wise counsel, good advice, moral understanding, rationale. Articulation, eloquence.

If the Mage of Swords represents a person: Judiciary, lawyer, litigant, military or civilian officer. Doctor, editor, lawmaker, or politician. Diplomat, scientist. Disciplinarian, dean or principal.

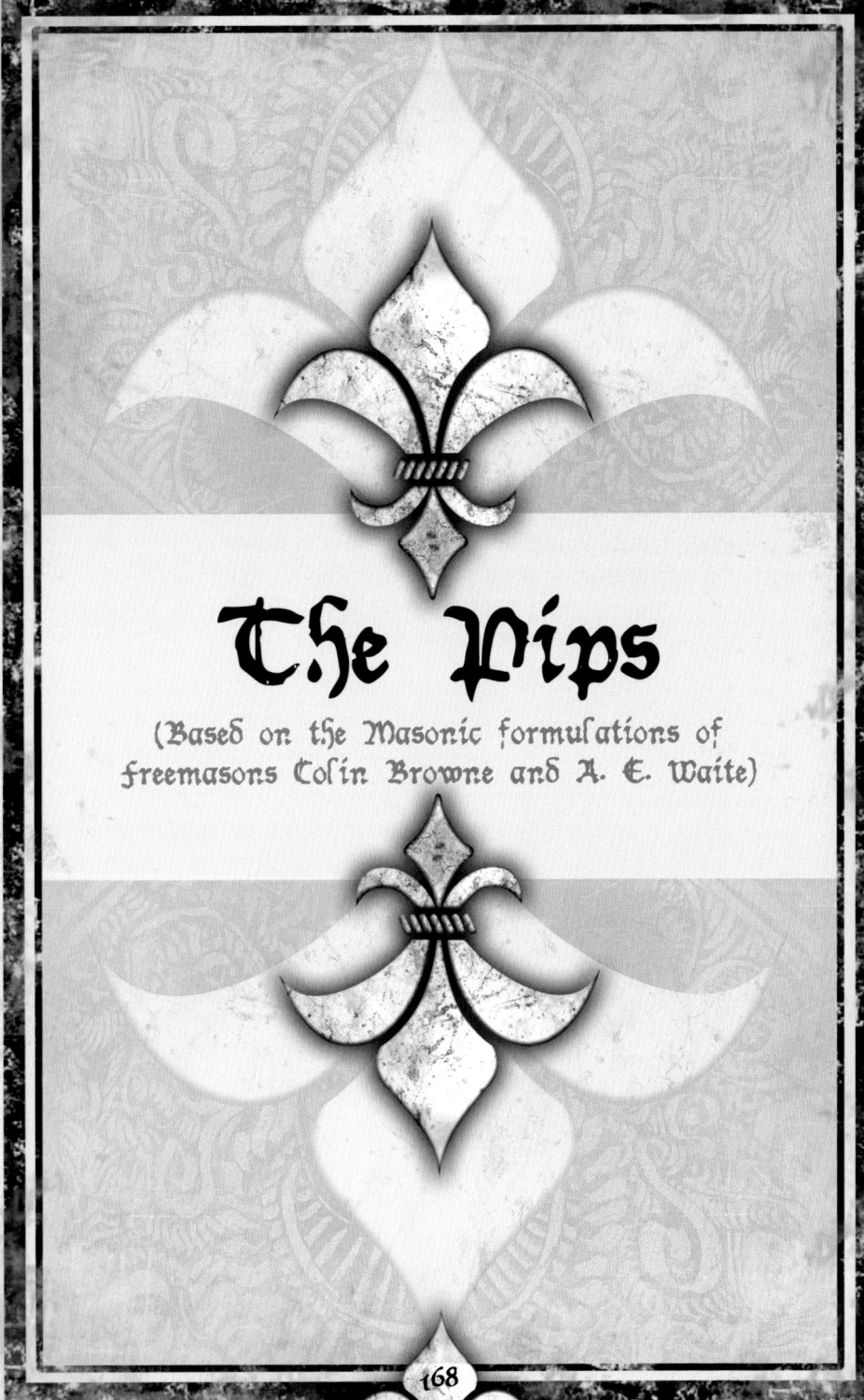

The Pips

(Based on the Masonic formulations of freemasons Colin Browne and A. E. Waite)

Ace of Swords

Trouble, opposition begins to brew. New problems. The birth of new solutions, conceptions of new ideas. Authority, victory, glory. Realization of newly found courage.

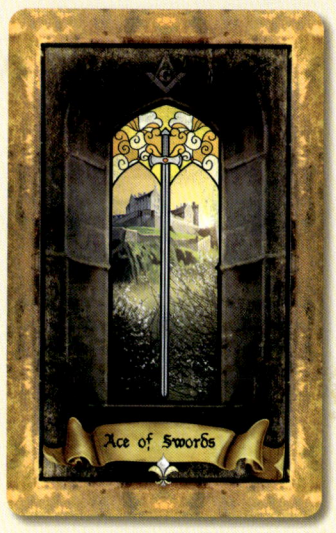

Two of Swords

Opposition to commencement, anxiety regarding fresh starts, missed opportunities. Refusal to recognize problems, unable to make decisions. Situations require bravery and daring.

Three of Swords

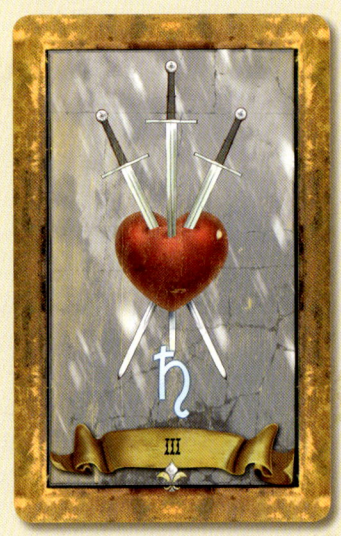

Recognition of hostility and opposition. Divorce, separation, estrangement. Incomatibility. Arguments, disagreements. Absence, delay, division. Alienation, disaffection.

Four of Swords

Love succeeds against hatred, opposition, and enemies. Vigilance, solitude, contemplation. Ideas triumph where actions fail. Meditation, rest, repose, retreat, refuge.

Five of Swords

Clash of ideas. Unexpected events lead to forfeiture, loss. Opposition triumphs. Degradation, distress. Not a good time to enter into new ventures. Misfortune, adversity, injury.

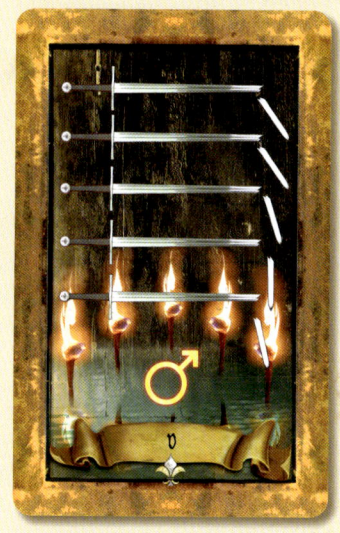

Six of Swords

Neutralizing of negative forces, effort results in expedient success. Journey to new opportunities—physically and/or psychologically. Means to a solution, pathway to resolution.

Seven of Swords

A losing battle, no options. Unattainable goals, wasted effort. Theft, betrayal, disappointment. Failed strategies, rethink positioning. Reclaim what was taken, renew lost faith.

Eight of Swords

Opposition partially successful. Annoyance, delay. Outdated methodology causes stagnation. Refusal to recognize obstacles. Imprisoned by one's own thinking and difficulties.

Nine of Swords

Ill will prevails for extended period of time. Deception, disillusionment. Disappointment, sorrow, ethical suffering, lack of integrity. Grief, guilt, remorse. Delayed relief, stalled answers.

Ten of Swords

Inexplicable opposition leads to pain, sadness, and failure. Loss of loved ones. Exhaustion, sudden hardship, downward changes. False friends, betrayal, shattered confidence. Mistrust.

Conclusion

The Grand Architect of the Universe blessed me mightily the day I was introduced to South African artiste extraordinaire Bob Greyvenstein. Referred to him by a fellow Tarotist friend on Facebook, Bob and I quickly became internet friends and artistic partners, sharing our thoughts and musings via cyberspace for this deck and book set. There I was, typing away in the wilds of South Dakota and Bob brought life to my ideas and words, employing his remarkable artistic magic from his home in Pretoria, South Africa. The very concept amazes me, that two individuals so many thousands of miles apart would never meet yet come together to create something wonderful.

Bob and I bring you what I know to be a truly unique Tarot; I guarantee there is nothing like it in the world of oracle mystery. Thank you for accepting our invitation to journey with us down the fork in the Royal Road and into the shadows of secret societies and the provocative notions of alternative history. I personally appreciate your willingness to give your valuable time to my theories as they are presented here; I was a little hesitant to lay them out for public viewing (who am I kidding—I was petrified). But, I do ascribe to the great Isaac Asimov: "Your assumptions are your Windows on the world. Scrub them off every once in a while, or the light won't come in."

Merci beaucoup. Profiter du voyage et la vue, mais prendre soin lorsque vous tournez!
—CASEY DUHAMEL

Bibliography

Baigent, Lincoln and Leigh. *HolyBlood, HolyGrail.* New York: Random House, 1982.

Childress, David Hatcher. *Pirates and the Lost Templar Fleet: The Secret Naval War Between the Templars & the Vatican.* Illinois: Adventures Unlimited Press, 2003.

Cicero, Chic and Sandra Tabatha. *The New Golden Dawn Ritual Tarot.* Minnesota: Llewellyn Publications, 1991.

Clifton, Chas S. *Encyclopedia of Heresies and Heretics.* New York: ABC-CLIO, 1992.

Fanthorpe, Lionel and Patricia. *Secrets of Rennes le Chateau: The Mysteries of Templar Treasure, Rosicrucians, and the Holy Grail.* Massachusetts: Weiser Books, 1992.

Decker, Ronald. *The Esoteric Tarot.* Illinois: Quest Books, 2013.

Greer, Mary K. *The Complété Book of Tarot Reversais.* Minnesota: Llewellyn Publications, 2002.

Greer, Mary K. *Women of the Golden Dawn.* Vermont: Park Street Press, 1995.

Greer, Mary K. and Tom Little. *Understanding the Tarot Court.* Minnesota: Llewellyn Publications, 2004.

Hall, Manly P. *The Secret Teachings of All Ages: Masonic, Hermetic, Qabbalistic & Rosicrucian Philosophy.* The Philosophical Research Society, 1988.

Howells, Robert. *Inside the Priory of Sion*. London, England: Watkins Publishing, 2011.

Karg, Barb and Rick Sutherland. *Secret America: The Hidden Symbols, Codes, and Mysteries of the United States*. Massachusetts: Adams Media, 2010.

Macoy, Robert. *A Dictionary of Freemasonry*. New York: Random House, 1989.

Mann, William E. *The Knights Templar in the New World*. Massachusetts: Destiny Books, 2004.

O'Shea, Stephen. *The Perfect Heresy: The Revolutionary Life and Death of the Medieval Cathars*. New York: Walker Publishing Company, Inc., 2000.

Papus. *The Divinatory Tarot*. London, England: Aeon Books, 2008.

Papus. *The Tarot of the Bohemians*. London, England: George Redway, 1896.

Payne-Towler, Christine. *The Underground Stream: Esoteric Tarot Revealed*. Oregon: Noreah Press, 1999.

Picknett, Lynn and Clive Prince. *The Templar Revelation: Secret Guardians of the True Identity of Christ*. New York: Touchstone, 1997.

Place, Robert M. *The Tarot: History, Symbolism, and Divination*. New York: The Penguin Group, 2005.

Pollack, Rachel. *Seventy-Eight Degrees of Wisdom: A Book of Tarot*. London, England: Thorsons, 1997.

Robinson, John J. *Born In Blood: The Lost Secrets of Freemasonry*. New York: M. Evans and Co., Inc., 1989.

Sora, Steven. *The Lost Colony of the Templars*. Massachusetts: Destiny Books, 2004.

Starbird, Margaret. *The Tarot Trumps and the Holy Grail: Great Secrets of the Middle Ages*. Colorado: Wovenword Press, 2000.

Swiryn, Robert. *The Secret of the Tarot*. Pau Hana Publishing, 2010.